Homesteading in Urban U.S.A.

Anne Clark
Zelma Rivin

Homesteading in Urban U.S.A.

PRAEGER SPECIAL STUDIES IN U.S. ECONOMIC, SOCIAL, AND POLITICAL ISSUES

Praeger Publishers   New York   London

Library of Congress Cataloging in Publication Data

Clark, Anne, 1939-
    Homesteading in urban U.S.A.

    (Praeger special studies in U.S. economic, social,
and political issues)
    Bibliography: p.
    1. Urban homesteading—United States—Cast studies.
I. Rivin, Zelma, 1921-   joint author. II. Title.
HD7293.C58   301.5'4   77-2926
ISBN 0-275-24060-6

PRAEGER PUBLISHERS
200 Park Avenue, New York, N.Y. 10017, U.S.A.

Published in the United States of America in 1977
by Praeger Publishers, Inc.

789   038   987654321

Printed in the United States of America

ACKNOWLEDGMENTS

We would like to acknowledge the assistance we received in preparing this study. Dr. Wolfgang Pindur, director of urban studies program, Old Dominion University, was project adviser. He was available for consultation at all times. We are indebted for his advice and guidance. Dr. Beverly Bryant, assistant dean, School of Arts and Letters, Old Dominion University, counseled and corrected. Dr. Donald Smith, assistant professor of sociology, Old Dominion University, helped with data processing programs. A grant from the graduate studies department provided the funds for on-site inspections of three urban homestead programs. The homestead directors in those three cities contributed their knowledge and experience and personally accompanied our tours. Mr. Roger Windsor of Baltimore's Home Ownership Program, Mr. Theodore Spaulding of Wilmington's homestead office, and Messrs. Moore and Brooks of the homestead office in Hospitality House, Washington, D.C., were helpful and enthusiastic about our project. Ms. Jacquie Brenner of the AFL-CIO Housing Department has been a frequent correspondent and source of information. Mr. James Banks, executive director of the Greater Washington Board of Realtors, arranged for us to contact some homestead officials in Washington. Congressman Robert Daniel's office helped us gain entree to some Washington officials. Congresswoman Holt's office set up a meeting with the Department of Housing and Urban Development (HUD). Delegate Robert Washington, Virginia state legislature, provided information regarding Virginia's housing status. Ms. Eva Teig, director, Office of Economic Analysis and Planning, City of Portsmouth, Virginia, pretested the homesteading officials' schedule. We would like to thank Mr. Bob Metrakos, executive director of the chamber of commerce, for follow-up letters to the chamber directors. Mr. Bart Frye of the Portsmouth Redevelopment and Housing Authority (PRHA) provided many articles. The PRHA library and staff were very helpful.

The time and effort put into the preparation of this study were spent largely at the expense of our husbands and families. We are grateful for their support. Special thanks to Dorothy Shelby for baby-sitting.

CONTENTS

Page

ACKNOWLEDGMENTS   v

LIST OF TABLES   x

Chapter

1 INTRODUCTION   1

    Notes   5

2 THEORETICAL FRAMEWORK   6

    Background of Problems   6
      Abandonment   6
      Finance   8
      Neighborhood Stability   11
      Housing Needs   12
    Homeownership Theory   15
    Notes   17

3 PREVIOUS WRITINGS ON HOMESTEADING   20

    History and Theory   20
    Government Participation   26
    Criticism and Guidelines   30
    Notes   33

4 RESEARCH METHODS AND PROCEDURES   36

    Defining the Universe   36
    Hypotheses   37
    Schedules and Populations   39
    Survey   41
    Presentation of Data   44
    Note   45

5 CASE STUDY ANALYSIS OF HOMESTEADING
   IN 11 CITIES   46

Baltimore, Maryland   47
   Background   47
   Unique Characteristics   48
   Laws and Administration   49
   Financial Options   50
   Support Services   51
   Benefits to City   51
   Benefits to Homesteader   52
Buffalo, New York   52
   Background   52
   Unique Characteristics   56
   Laws and Administration   56
   Financial Options   57
   Support Services   57
   Benefits   57
Camden, New Jersey   57
   Background   57
   Unique Characteristics   59
   Laws and Administration   59
   Financial Options and Support Services 60
   Benefits   61
Minneapolis, Minnesota   62
   Background   62
   Unique Characteristics   63
   Laws and Administration   63
   Financial Options   65
   Support Services   65
   Benefits   65
Newark, New Jersey   68
   Background   68
   Unique Characteristics   68
   Laws and Administration   69
   Benefits   69
Philadelphia, Pennsylvania   71
   Background   71
   Unique Characteristics   72
   Laws and Administration   74
   Financial Options   75
   Support Services   75
   Benefits   77
Pittsburgh, Pennsylvania   77
   Background   77
   Unique Characteristics   78
   Laws and Administration   78
   Financial Options   79

Support Services 79
Benefits 79
Rockford, Illinois 81
Background 81
Unique Characteristics 82
Laws and Administration 82
Financial Options 83
Support Services 83
Benefits 84
St. Louis, Missouri 86
Background 86
Unique Characteristics 87
Laws and Administration 87
Benefits 90
Washington, D.C. 90
Background 90
Unique Characteristics 91
Laws and Administration 91
Financial Options 92
Support Services 92
Benefits 93
Wilmington, Delaware 95
Background 95
Unique Characteristics 97
Laws and Administration 97
Financial Options 98
Support Services 98
Benefits 99
Notes 107

6 STATISTICAL ANALYSIS OF HOMESTEADING
ACCORDING TO AFFECTED GROUPS 111

Civic Leaders 112
Hypothesis I 112
Hypothesis II 114
Hypothesis III 116
Homestead Officials 117
Hypothesis I 118
Hypothesis II 120
Hypothesis III 122
Homesteaders 124
Hypothesis I 127
Hypothesis II 129
Hypothesis III 131

      Hypothesis IV   136
      Hypothesis V   141
   Notes   143

7 CONCLUSION   144

   City Analysis   144
      Goals   145
      Administrative Structure   145
      Program Implementation   145
   Statistical Analysis   146
      Civic Leaders   146
      Officials   146
      Homesteaders   147
   Synthesis   147
      Cities   147
      Program   148
      Problems   150
      Benefits   150
   Implications   151
      Policy Implementation Research   151
      Policy Evaluation Research   152
   Notes   154

Appendix

A STAGES OF URBAN HOMESTEADING PROGRAMS   155

B SCHEDULES   156

SELECTED BIBLIOGRAPHY   166

ABOUT THE AUTHORS   181

LIST OF TABLES

Table		Page
4.1	Questionnaire Returns	43
5.1	Comparative Data for Baltimore	53
5.2	Baltimore, Maryland Homesteader Path, REAL Loan and Conventional Loans	54
5.3	Baltimore, Maryland Homesteader Path, 312 Loan Property (Stirling Street)	54
5.4	Baltimore, Maryland City Path, REAL Loan and Conventional Loans	55
5.5	Comparative Data for Buffalo	58
5.6	Buffalo, New York Homesteader Path	58
5.7	Buffalo, New York City Path	58
5.8	Comparative Data for Camden	61
5.9	Camden, New Jersey Homesteader Path	61
5.10	Camden, New Jersey City Path	61
5.11	Comparative Data for Minneapolis	66
5.12	Minneapolis, Minnesota Homesteader Path	67
5.13	Minneapolis, Minnesota City Path	67
5.14	Census Data for Newark	70
5.15	Newark, New Jersey Homesteader Path	70
5.16	Newark, New Jersey City Path	70
5.17	Comparative Data for Philadelphia	76
5.18	Philadelphia, Pennsylvania Homesteader Path	76
5.19	Philadelphia, Pennsylvania City Path	76
5.20	Comparative Data for Pittsburgh	80
5.21	Pittsburgh, Pennsylvania Homesteader Path	80
5.22	Pittsburgh, Pennsylvania City Path	80
5.23	Comparative Data for Rockford	85
5.24	Rockford, Illinois Homesteader Path	85
5.25	Rockford, Illinois City Path	85
5.26	Comparative Data for St. Louis	89
5.27	St. Louis, Missouri Homesteader Path	89
5.28	St. Louis, Missouri City Path	89
5.29	Comparative Data for Washington	94
5.30	Washington, D.C. Homesteader Path	94
5.31	Washington, D.C. City Path	94
5.32	Comparative Data for Wilmington	101
5.33	Wilmington, Delaware Homesteader Path	101
5.34	Wilmington, Delaware City Path	101
5.35	Comparison of City Program Structure	102
5.36	Comparison of Abandoned Housing Conditions	103
5.37	Comparison of Homestead Units	104
5.38	Comparison of Homesteading Requirements	105

5.39	Comparison of Support Services	106
5.40	Comparison of Program Problems	107
6.1	Distribution of Benefits to the City as Seen by Civic Leaders	114
6.2	Number of Homesteads According to Type of Agency	119
6.3	Problems Encountered According to Number of Homesteads as Reported by Homestead Officials	120
6.4	Possible Homesteading Adaptations According to Officials	123
6.5	Socioeconomic Description of Homesteaders	126
6.6	Opportunity for Homeownership	129
6.7	Homesteader Problems According to Income	131
6.8	Loan Source According to Income	133
6.9	Income According to Race among Homesteaders	134
6.10	Homesteader Satisfaction as Related to Problem Identification	137
6.11	Satisfaction with Program According to Finance Method	139
6.12	Homestead Neighborhoods as Perceived by Homesteaders	141

Homesteading in Urban U.S.A.

The concept of homesteading has existed in the United States since 1842. It is only since 1973 that this concept has been adapted for urban use. Since then it has created widespread interest from all segments of society. Urban homesteading was developed as one of several policies designed to confront two urgent and growing problems of U.S. cities, housing abandonment and neighborhood deterioration. These two problems seem to be affecting the economy and vitality of cities as well as citizens. Urban homesteading is based on the theory that homeownership and housing rehabilitation can intervene successfully to reverse the trend of growing abandonment and blight. The program attempts to recycle vacant, deteriorated, and abandoned houses that are the product of neighborhood disinvestment.

A city has three options: It can remove these houses, allow them to remain unimproved, or adopt a policy to rehabilitate them. Removal or demolition is an expensive procedure. Not only are dollars spent by this process, but much needed shelter for an underhoused population is lost as well. The vacant land that is created by demolition often remains vacant and unproductive. The option of nondecision, or allowing the abandoned houses to remain unimproved, is very costly. The dollar cost of maintenance, surveillance, and fire service is high. The hidden cost is also high: Vacant homes encourage crime; vacant homes reduce the value of nearby properties and often encourage their abandonment; abandoned homes make no contribution to a city's tax base. The third option, rehabilitating abandoned housing, has been approached in a variety of ways. Urban homesteading is one policy of rehabilitation that is being explored in U.S. cities in order to ease the national housing shortage, the high rate of housing abandonment, and various manifestations of neighborhood deterioration. These problems are now considered items of national priority, as we can see in the Community Development Act.[1]

Mayor Thomas Maloney of Wilmington, Delaware, the first U.S. city to undertake urban homesteading, was perplexed by this dilemma. "Wilmington has 2,000 unproductive abandoned homes," he said, "so why not give them away?"[2] That is just what urban homesteading purports to do: "give away" for one dollar a deteriorated or abandoned dwelling on the condition that the donee will repair it and live in it. In this way a unit of housing is retained and restored to the tax roles, and a family is provided with shelter and homeownership.

The idea is intriguing and apparently simple. It immediately provoked the interest of the media, which headlined its inception. Some thoughtful writers foresaw problems for the city and pitfalls for eager citizen homesteaders. Many claims have been made about homesteading; some have heralded it as a salvation for cities, while others have decried it as more romance than reality. Much published material is of propaganda nature. It seems apparent that there is a need to discover the facts. Dr. George Sternlieb of Rutgers University underscored this need in a paper presented to a housing conference in 1974. "As yet urban homesteading is a phrase in search of a program, its success measured by public relations handouts rather than families housed."[3]

We hope to find out about urban homesteading on several levels. The first area of concern is where the policy should originate and who should be responsible for its implementation and funding. To date, all urban-homestead programs have resulted from city ordinances or city administrative decisions. The state and federal governments have not initiated any legal framework for urban homesteading. Section 810 of the Community Development Act is a provision for an experiment in urban homesteading that will be implemented by the U.S. Department of Housing and Urban Development (HUD).[4] Regional and state planning has not concerned itself with this policy to any great extent. The role of government as it affects urban homesteading needs clarification. A second issue concerns the goals of urban homesteading. Our literature review indicates that some theorists and scholars believe urban homesteading should function as a method of neighborhood stabilization and that in order to fulfill this role the program should include in-depth social services and should focus on those who need housing most. Others view urban homesteading as a housing program that will recycle houses and enhance a city's tax base. Should urban homesteading play an economic or a social role? Is it a housing program or a neighborhood stabilization program? Or is it both? A third level of interest lies within the program itself. We want to know what the legal and financial problems are and how some cities are handling them. We need to know what it costs to get the program going and keep it going, how many houses can actually be brought into such a program, and how much it costs the city and the citizens to do it. Are these houses really one dollar albatrosses as George Sternlieb fears?[5] We need to know how the people who have become homesteaders feel about it. Is it worth the huge investment of their time, effort, and money? Will the houses be worth what they have put into them? Will the restoration of these houses help neighborhood revitalization?

The nature of urban homesteading probably explains why no serious studies have been attempted. Most programs require an occupancy period of two to five years before the homesteader becomes a homeowner. As of this writing, the occupancy requirement has not been fulfilled in any city. No homesteader has had time to complete the minimum living requirement and to acquire clear title to his property. This time factor imposes severe limitations on any effort to analyze urban homesteading. It is difficult to tell whether homestead neighborhoods are changing direction, whether homesteaders become more satisfied citizens, whether cities increase their tax base, or whether the houses will resell at a profit. In addition the size of the program limits the student. The program is very small. In most cities it is designed as a pilot program and is in its initial stages. It is difficult to measure the effects of a small program on a large problem with any degree of significance.

Nevertheless, there is a need for study now; there is an urgency to the problem of housing abandonment and neighborhood deterioration. If city planners and decision makers delay until a full-scale evaluation is available to them, they must ignore a very volatile and costly situation. Many houses that are now repairable may be lost to vandalism and decay. Neighboring properties that are now occupied may become abandoned. Cities may lose a good opportunity. A study now could aid cities that are considering the program as well as cities that are already engaged in the program. A study now could reveal certain facts about homesteaders that may not be available at a later date. It seems logical to assume that homesteaders are presently under great financial and personal stress. Therefore an investigation into the areas of their satisfaction or dissatisfaction at this time might be more realistic than later, when the homesteaders are further removed from the problems. Such an investigation at this time might reveal areas of program weakness that would be ignored later. A final reason for studying homesteading at this time is that the data acquired now can help in the design of future studies. Cities that want to write evaluation studies into their program will be aided by the information this study provides.

This study of urban homesteading has two main purposes: to enlarge on some descriptive studies that have been done on urban homesteading

and to analyze data collected from three categories of actors who
are affected by the program. The previous studies were limited by
time and by the scope of the policy. They described only the first few
cities that implemented it. This study will include a descriptive
analysis of 11 cities that had urban-homestead programs in June 1975.
It will use new materials and data for this analysis. Now that urban
homesteading exists in at least 11 cities, it seems logical to make
some comparison among them. Some studies have been concerned
with problems, mainly the legal and financial problems of implementation. No study of benefits has been conducted. The benefits have
been treated in the mass media and are generally impressionistic
in nature. No attempt has been made to gather empirical data on
problems or benefits as they are perceived by the homesteaders
themselves, by program officials, or by other citizens.

To our knowledge, no study has covered the material used in
this work. Therefore, the authors have set out with the intention
of presenting heretofore unknown data. It is hoped that this book
will provide some scientific basis for decision making about urban-
homesteading policy and the implementation of that policy.

The study is divided into two main parts: a descriptive analysis
of 11 urban homestead programs and a statistical analysis of data
gathered from three survey questionnaires. The descriptive analysis
of cities includes the background, unique characteristics, legal and
administrative structures, financial options, support services, and
benefits of each urban-homestead program. It also includes, for
each city, a chart describing the administration path and the homesteader path from inception to completion of the program. The statistical analysis includes findings based on 14 hypotheses derived
from the theories and goals of the programs. These hypotheses were
developed into three questionnaire schedules, which were designed
to produce the data for the analysis. The conclusion presents a
synthesis of these two sections and a design for an evaluative study
to be conducted in the future.

We believe this study is important. It is important for an understanding of urban homesteading as a housing program, and it is
important for a better understanding of the role of rehabilitation in
neighborhood revitalization. A clarification of the parameters and
limitations of urban homesteading, as well as its possibilities, may
lead to more realistic expectations and less romanticizing. We hope
that the facts we present may help cities to make more rational
decisions about housing problems.

NOTES

1. U.S. Congress, House, Housing and Community Development Act of 1974, 93rd Cong., 1974, pp. 1-2.

2. Wayne King, "Homesteaders Combating Urban Blight," New York Times, 16 September 1973, p. A 1.

3. George Sternlieb, The Myth and Potential Reality of Urban Homesteading (New Brunswick, N.J.: Rutgers University, Center for Urban Policy Research, 1974), p. 1.

4. Housing and Community Development Act of 1974, op. cit., p. 101.

5. George Sternlieb, letter to authors, April 8, 1975.

2

THEORETICAL
FRAMEWORK

The concept of urban homesteading has been introduced by several different authors on the basis of different urban-related theories. The theory that is central to the program is homeownership. Urban homesteading promotes homeownership, primarily. In the process, it puts abandoned houses to use; it improves neighborhoods; it improves city tax returns, and it houses people. The other theories relate to urban problems present in cities adopting the concept as a policy. They include abandonment, neighborhood stability, housing needs, and urban finance. These will be discussed first as the background of problems prompting an urban-homesteading policy. The theory of homeownership will be explained as a means to alleviate these problems.

BACKGROUND OF PROBLEMS

Abandonment

The common sight of uninhabited, unserviced structures rapidly deteriorating through neglect and vandalism has reached levels of great concern in many large cities, with no end in sight. This has occurred despite government efforts at turning or, at least, stemming the tide through recent legislation. In New York City 100,000 units are abandoned; in Philadelphia there are 30,000.[1] St. Louis has 10,000 with 16 percent of the structures abandoned in some neighborhoods.[2] In Chicago's Lawndale area, 20 percent of the structures are abandoned.[3] Baltimore had approximately 4,000 such units in 1970.[4] These figures are repeated all over the nation: Los Angeles, New Orleans, Oakland, Omaha, Milwaukee, Atlanta, and Houston are only a few of the most affected cities. The type of structure and the numbers abandoned vary with local conditions, but the process is present in both old and relatively new cities and in cities of both high multi-unit structures and high single-family dwellings. The Department of Housing and Urban Development is the owner of many of these structures by default. As of June 1973 it owned 202,811 housing units, and the total was expected to increase 50 percent by June 1975.[5]

The process of abandonment is obscure and complex, involving the interaction of social, political, and economic forces. Several different theories have been proposed as an explanation of the phenomenon. The causes of abandonment—initiators and propellants— are difficult to separate from the effects. Stoloff's study, "The National Survey of Housing Abandonment," cites exploitative practices by real-estate interests that take advantage of short-term opportunities for overcrowding as a cause.[6] Other factors include decreased maintenance, increased rents, increased sales prices, and disinvestment by lending agencies. This is coupled with recent trends toward social and economic grouping by blacks into middle and low income neighborhoods that are all black. Urban renewal, high taxes, and code enforcement were found to exacerbate but not to cause abandonment.

Sternlieb found that discrimination against minorities, housing crowding, and low-income tenants with female heads of households were significant factors in abandonment.[7] The inflated sales price as well as urban renewal are serious factors in, but not the cause of, abandonment. There is a cyclical effect of the owner-tenancy economics, and the owner responds by disinvestment. According to Sternlieb, "The impact of the decline in value cannot be overstated in accounting for owner insecurity in improving parcels."[8]

Many housing economists contended that new construction exceeded demand during the past decade and resulted in a downward pressure on the prices of existing units. The downward pressure plus the lower rate of inflation in older units spurred the filtering process of houses down the income ladder. Better houses became available, and the worst housing stock was abandoned.

However the process is described, the elements present in a "crisis ghetto," where abandonment is most evident, are "decreasing family incomes, increasing unemployment, increasing number of female-headed households, declining total population, increasing public assistance dependency, and increasing rates of crime and vandalism."[9] The process occurs to both sound and deteriorating structures in an affected area. The survey quoted above discovered that the tipping point, when abandonment becomes visible, occurs when 3 to 6 percent of the structures are abandoned. The causes

and the presence of abandonment are not the physical characteristics
of the building, according to Sternlieb. He found that, "Residential
abandonment seems to be much more a function of tax delinquency,
owner-tenant interplay, and neighborhood location than of physical
characteristics of the building itself."[10] The process is slow, con-
fused, and seemingly irreversible.

Several barriers to abandonment were identified, however, in
the Sternlieb and National Survey studies. Sternlieb concluded that
"any measure which would improve the relationship between the
renter and the owner, increase owner-occupancy, and curtail transiency would retard abandonment."[11] The owner-occupancy variable,
used in his analysis of factors predicting a decrease in abandonment,
was the strongest predictor of a decrease of abandonment. It was
much stronger than any of the other variables used. The factors
operating as barriers that were identified by the National Survey study
were a high rate of single-family homeownership; continuing homeownership investment; a relatively substantial and dispersed black
middle class; and the willingness of financial institutions to commit
mortgages in all sections of the city at uninflated rates.[12]

The field of abandonment research is conclusive on the extent of
the problem, the elements present in the most advanced abandoned
neighborhoods, and the various factors affecting the process. The
exact interplay of these factors is still being theorized, but certain
ones have been identified that both accelerate and hinder the process.
Abandonment itself is a symptom of another, equally serious urban
problem, the problem of financing the city.

                                   Finance

There is high demand for low-income housing because of its
small supply. The market operates by increasing the price of the
housing to meet the demand. The demand (low-income persons)
cannot meet the high prices except by crowding. This raises the
cost per unit for the owner, reducing the profitability. As the profitability falls, the resale value tends to decline. The possibility of
acquiring financing by mortgate lenders to improve the property
in hopes of recouping the initial investment is lessened as the mortgage lenders "redline" an area of questionable returns on the loan.
A redlined district is an area of marginal maintenance that has been
determined by the capital market as too risky for investment. Conventional improvement loans are unobtainable for residents in this
area. The owner, with no recourse to lenders or to increased rent,
discontinues maintenance of the property. This disinvestment
process continues until the structure is finally completely abandoned

by the owner, the tenants, and the city. This in turn will produce
an increased demand for low-income housing. Higher prices and
more crowding result as the process repeats itself over and over
again on structure after structure.

Real-estate investments are based on long-term capital gains as
the value appreciates. Since an investor is striving to maximize the
rates of return during the time that he has the property, he will
invest where the capital gains offer the most return. Since the low-
income housing market does not appreciate in value normally and the
only tax advantages for this market have been to owners claiming
depreciation, low investment and high rent are the only means of
compensation to owners for their initial investment. Normally,
current cash returns account for less than one-third of the overall
returns of real-estate investments. However, this is all that slum
owners have for returns. Because the amount of rent would have
to be increased so much to assure a rate of return comparable with
other areas of investment, low-income investors cannot compete
with others in the money-lending market or invest their own money
and remain in the low-income housing market. Michael Stegman
summed this up:

> Current cash returns to inner-city real estate are just
> about the only return that these dubious assets now yield,
> since there are few opportunities for appreciation and
> capital gains, and tax savings from deducting depreciation
> allowances from income are low. Add to this the greater
> than average liquidity of the assets, the risks and un-
> certainties of maintaining positive cash flows over extend-
> ed periods, the high level of management skills required
> for satisfactory performance and the hostile environment
> of the inner-city market, and it becomes clear why inves-
> tors demand current returns upward of 25 percent before
> they will commit their resources to additional invest-
> ments.[13]

This disinvestment process in the inner city affects the city's
income. Property taxes are assessed on the value of the property.
With no access to the lending market, property and, subsequently,
property taxes decline. The suburban flight of upper- and middle-
income persons, followed by the businesses catering to them, also
diminishes city tax returns. But if the suburbs are taxable by the
city, services must be extended to them.

Municipal expenditures for services decrease per capita with an
increase in population. The denser the population, the lower the
costs per capita. If the increase in population is spread out, as in

the suburbs, the expenditures do no decrease as expected. If, in
addition, there is a decrease in the population of the once-dense
inner city, per capita expenditures increase. This decrease may
result in a decline in the taxable population. Hence, the inner city
may become more expensive to service. The demand for services
is high in the new suburban areas, and the city responds by diver-
sifying its allocations to a broader spectrum of services. The
inefficient distribution of land use is a cost to a community when it
must extend services and facilities to formless suburban and
exurban areas. Neither the inner city nor the suburb can be efficiently
served. This conclusion was supported by Kasarda in a study of
suburban impact on city services. [14] The broader range of types of
services demanded and the broader area to be serviced result in
higher costs in distribution of city services to suburbs than to the
central city. It holds true for all services measured, public and
private. This is sometimes partially offset by sales tax and employment. The costs of suburbs to a city are often overlooked when
considering the costs of maintaining the inner city. The result is a
growing financial problem for city governments trying to serve two
groups with less dense population.

The redlining of deteriorating neighborhoods affects inner-city
businesses as well as residences. Without government intervention
requiring all lenders to take the same risks, the market does not
operate in a way to allow such risks. Such legislation is presently
under consideration. Without the necessary funds, urban areas
disintegrate. With the funds, the economics of renovation are still
risky for the individual: If the owner improves his property, he
may possibly gain a 10 percent rate of return. [15] This would be
based on the catalytic effect that would cause other neighbors to
invest in renovation of their property, also. If other owners did not
improve their property, the investing owner would probably receive
only a 3 percent rate of return. If neither owner invests, he might
receive a 5 percent rate of return at least, and the largest rate
would be infinite (a term to indicate that any return would be positive since no investment has been made). In blighted neighborhoods
owners assume that their neighbors will not invest, given the market
discouragement of renovation. In this uncertain climate, the rational
investor will not improve his property. If he is upwardly mobile,
he will move to another neighborhood. In this kind of situation, called
the "prisoner's dilemma," the value of a commodity is related to
another commodity. Property value is tied to its area. A homeowner
who invests in property improvements may recoup those costs only
if his neighbor also improves. The only solution is a neighborhood
decision not to maximize their rate of return in the short run but to
agree to invest so that all have a vested interest in the stability of

the neighborhood. They may still be unable to borrow from the capital market, but the decision to redline seems based on whether one thinks the neighborhood is blighted. If one thinks that it is blighted, lenders will not loan money and the neighborhood becomes blighted. This compounds the problem of neighborhood stability.

Neighborhood Stability

The process of neighborhood deterioration has been observed and studied frequently, as have neighborhoods that have stabilized after showing a tendency toward blight.

Jane Jacobs describes the process of stabilization of a neighborhood as the increase of the diversity of land uses.[16] This has been practiced in Baltimore, Maryland, where local markets have been established throughout the city. Surrounding neighborhoods have seen a rebirth in activity and housing renovation.[17] The market is often used as a meeting ground for residents as they plan for desired changes in their neighborhoods.

Another Jacobs tenet for viable neighborhoods is a diversity in type of residents. This has been the one most difficult to establish, once a neighborhood is homogeneous, without total disruption of the neighborhood pattern. It has been accomplished through concerted efforts in several locations, however. Julia Abrahamson compares the neighborhood with incipient blight to a stable area with goals and self-initiated improvements.[18]

A well-organized community group led Chicago's Hyde Park-Kenwood to become a strong, integrated community. The community group, or neighborhood organization, was the motivating factor in another such process in South Shore in Chicago. Harvey Molotch reported that a strong community group with the goal of a stable, biracial neighborhood was able to reverse a trend toward blight.[19]

In Norfolk, Virginia, such processes of maintaining stability have occurred in Colonial Place and in Ballentine Place.[20] In a study of Colonial Place in Norfolk, Virginia, neighborhood interest was found to be very strong.[21] This was particularly true of homeowners. Interest in the neighborhood organization was high. Millspaugh and Breckenfeld discuss the changes outside the neighborhood.[22] They see politicians treating once-blighted neighborhoods with new respect. The extent of this change varies in direct ratio with the power of the neighborhood organization.

Neighborhoods without this aid to stability still seem to have a strong sense of community. One of the detrimental effects of urban-renewal projects was the sense of loss produced in the relocatees, the persons whose homes were acquired by the government for other purposes. Housing must be located for these residents by the government. In some cities they are offered priority for homesteading. Relocatees had a sense of loss even when their new situation was a physical improvement. Jacobs described this loyalty to the community in West End in Boston prior to its demolition. Marc Fried and Peggy Gleicher came to similar conclusions from their study of West End.[23] Local people and places provided a framework for personal and social integration. A similar neighborhood was the focus of a study by Jeffrey Solomon, with similar results found in a sense of community being present.[24]

These last two studies were conducted on more homogeneous groups of low-income people. Jacobs might see that as an explanation of why their neighborhoods, while fulfilling certain psychological and social needs of the residents, were not as viable as other areas of their respective cities. Roderick McKenzie, however, found in a study of neighborhoods that neighborhood sentiment thrives best where population is homogeneous and stable and has a high percentage of homeownership.[25]

Whatever the mix of the neighborhood, it seems clear that the needs of the residents are best served when the neighborhoods are preserved. Rehabilitation is not only less expensive than new housing, but it helps preserve the fabric of social life built by the residents. It utilizes existing housing stock to help meet housing needs, another urban problem of large proportions.

Housing Needs

The nature of the nation's housing problem is both qualitative and quantitative. In 1970 approximately 7.8 million families could not afford a "decent home."[26] Of these families, 56 percent were living in the city. By 1978, 60 percent of the families who need housing assistance will be urban dwellers.

The minimum number of housing units that will need to be produced or rehabilitated in the United States by 1978 is 26 million units to reach the present housing goal.[27] There will still be 5 million substandard housing units in the United States by 1980. The inner-city slum dweller may be spending 30 to 35 percent of the family income for housing, as compared with 15 to 25 percent for the average family.[28]

The federal government has been concerned with the housing need of Americans since F.D. Roosevelt proclaimed the goal of "a decent home for every American." The attempt to fulfill this goal has been the stimulus behind every housing act. The Douglas report for the National Commission on Urban Problems, made in 1968, found that the conditions for housing the underhoused had not improved since 1960. [29] It is also reported that government action through urban renewal, highway programs, demolitions on public-housing sites, code enforcement, and other programs has destroyed more housing for the poor than government at all levels has built for them. After 30 years of involvement in housing, according to real-estate and housing reporter Joseph P. Fried, the various programs have produced a net total of approximately 1.5 million housing units, 14 percent of the need found to exist by the Douglas report. [30]

The Housing Act of 1949 incorporated the goal of "a decent home and a suitable living environment for every American family" with a plan for slum clearance and construction of public housing. [31] This was the era after World War II when many families needed housing, when the suburbs were mushrooming, and when automobiles became more available. As the cities expanded and the tax base moved farther out, housing filtered down. The process was accelerated by the urban-renewal projects of slum clearance. [32] The program was designed to eradicate blight, slums, and decay; but in many instances it merely accelerated these conditions. As structures were destroyed, the price of the remaining housing rose. The poor had to move outward and crowd into a narrow band beyond their former housing area. The urban-renewal program provided parcels of land to be assimilated for public use, such as hospitals and libraries. These necessary buildings and the readjustments in land use by assimilating parcels represent the successes of urban renewal. However, the dislocation that resulted from urban renewal was extensive. Rehabilitation was a part of the program but it did not receive a major emphasis.

The Housing Act of 1954 expanded the urban-renewal program and liberalized mortgage-insurance programs through the newly created Federal National Mortgage Association. [33] This program was aimed at stimulating housing credit and helping displaced families in urban-renewal areas. Blight continued to spread; and the number of housing units for low income declined. The Housing Act of 1961 shifted the emphasis to subsidizing the poor in mortgage-insurance programs and in rent payments. [34] This was extended in the Housing Act of 1964 to include the displaced urban-renewal families. [35] The 1964 act also included rehabilitation loans for urban-renewal areas. In 1965 a housing act was passed, creating the Department of Housing and Urban Development for more efficient management of the housing programs. [36]

The problem of housing was coming to be recognized as a more comprehensive problem than just the provision of housing. New housing projects did not seem to ensure stability in a neighborhood.

The social needs of a neighborhood are intertwined with the housing available. In order to allow some choice in housing for low income, rent subsidies and leasing arrangements were initiated. Federal Housing Administration (FHA) and Veterans Administration (VA) mortgages had provided some choice in housing, but middle-income groups had been the main beneficiaries. Subsidies and leasing arrangements allowed renters to spend 25 percent of their income and be subsidized for the rest of the cost of the rent. The lease arrangement allowed local housing authorities to lease privately owned units to low-income families eligible for public housing. In 1966 the Model Cities Program was created, allowing localities to design a comprehensive program of housing and services. [37] This plan called for citizen participation in every stage. The locally directed programs were for specific areas of the city, not for all neighborhoods or all citizens.

The Housing and Urban Development Act of 1968 aimed to provide a decent home for every American by 1978. [38] Section 1601 of the Act states:

> The Congress finds that the supply of the nation's housing is not increasing rapidly enough to meet the national housing goal, established in the Housing Act of 1949, of the 'realization as soon as feasible of the goal of a decent home and a suitable living environment for every American family.' The Congress reaffirms this national housing goal and determines that it can be substantially achieved within the next decade by the construction or rehabilitation of 26,000,000 housing units, 6,000,000 of these for low- and moderate-income families. [39]

Section 235, the homeownership-assistance program, was created to enable low-income persons to become homeowners. A subsidy sufficient to allow them to pay the equivalent of 1-percent interest on their mortgage was made available. Section 236 provided subsidies for the production of new multi-family units. Emphasis was placed on old, inner-city houses for rehabilitation by the poor. A large amount of collusion occurred between builders, realtors, and FHA officials which allowed many dilapidated and unsafe old homes to be given to the unsuspecting poor with no advice or means of improving the bad investment. [40] The concept of home-ownership and choice of location was unsuccessful in practice because a mechanism for assuring owner success and owner protection was missing. Later, it was realized that support services were essential to prevent fraudulent schemes against new, poor homeowners.

The Housing and Community Development Act of 1974 streamlined and combined the programs in existence to try to reach the poor more effectively. It combined the old categorical grants to provide community block grants. [41] The consolidation was passed in order to achieve a better use of the mortgage-insurance programs, better administration of the programs, and better evaluation of these programs. Urban homesteading is included in this act (Section 810). Support services and increased city services to the homestead site are the conditions for funding.

The federal acts from 1949 to the present are indicative of the developing theory of government intervention in the housing market, at both supply and demand ends of the market. The market has been found to be lacking in its provision of housing for low income; and it has been unable to utilize structures in neighborhoods with incipient blight. In order to meet the goal of a decent home for every American, the government has had to intervene. Most of the involvement has been at the federal level, which has the greatest resources for operating in the complex housing market. Recently, states have also begun to enter this field through state housing-study commissions (as in Virginia), state funding for rehabilitation (as in Minnesota), and state laws easing municipal acquisition of abandoned properties (as in Missouri).

HOMEOWNERSHIP THEORY

The urban problems of abandonment, declining financial bases, neighborhood deterioration, and housing needs are well-known facts in many U.S. cities. They are the backdrop of urban homesteading. Rehabilitation is the technique of providing the additional housing that urban homesteading offers. Homeownership theory is the rationale for the policy. Homeownership was cited earlier as a key barrier to abandonment. When property is occupied by owners, it is maintained better. The neighborhood is less likely to develop blight.

City finances are improved with increased homeownership and subsequent maintenance of property. Completely occupied neighborhoods are denser and therefore are more efficiently served by the city government than are scattered or blighted areas.

Neighborhood interest and pride is stronger among homeowners. A high percentage of owner-occupied houses indicates a stable neighborhood. Meeting housing needs includes recognizing social needs of residents. Maintaining the social ties or offering a choice of location develops neighborhoods. By utilizing substandard housing with the reward of homeownership, an attempt is being made to alleviate these urban problems.

Homeownership is a value deeply rooted in American tradition.
The original Homestead Act of 1862 was based on the belief that every
person had a right to a piece of the soil.[42] This is a basic investment
on which he or she could then build equity. Homeownership not only
provides shelter and perhaps a source of pride, but it is an "equity
accumulation device," according to Sternlieb.[43] Every study of
capital assets in the United States shows that the bulk of the people
have their major asset in the equity of their home. Most of their
wealth is tied to the house and lot that they have bought.

These very restraints help create the positive effects of homeownership for the neighborhood. Most tenants have less incentive
to boost their neighborhood, since all improvements become the
property of the landlord and are likely to mean higher rent. In addition, renting often indicates transiency without deep roots to the
neighborhood. Homeowners, on the other hand, have a built-in
incentive to better their surrounds, given the opportunity and knowledge. Neighborhoods with a high percentage of homeownership seem
a far more fertile field for rehabilitation than neighborhoods with a
high percentage of tenancy. Landlords have a built-in incentive to
perpetuate the slum effect of property-tax law and assessing practices. The landlord in residence is different. The relations with the
tenants are close; the landlord reacts like other homeowners.[44]

Because housing is such a visible commodity, people show more
concern for their neighbor's house than for his other more private
forms of consumption. Dilapidated housing is unsightly not just for
the owners but to neighbors as well. The dilapidated condition of a
house affects the dollar value of neighboring houses. This fact provides the rationale for public efforts at upgrading housing, particularly
that of the poor. The socially acceptable standard in housing is beyond
the reach of many poor families, either to rent or to buy. Assistance
through the demand side is easier to equalize, according to one report.[45] The largest federal housing program subsidizes demand
through tax breaks given to homeowners. The income-tax laws
strongly favor homeowners over renters. Under present tax policy,
nearly 60 percent of these tax concessions benefit families over
$20,000 income, and only 7 percent benefit families with incomes
under $10,000.[46]

Homeownership has the psychological advantage of extending
privacy. It tends to break the chains of dependency between tenants
and landlords. Owner-occupants are less likely to be forced out of
a house through a lack of code enforcement than renters. A study of
Baltimore tenants and homeowners was made by Stegman.[47] In a
comparison of the two groups, obvious differences were proven.
Mobility was much higher for renters. A relatively high number of the
moves of renters results from their being forced to move for reasons

beyond their control. Charles Adams has advocated homeownership as a key to improving quality and maintenance of the existing stock of inner-city houses. The data in Stegman's study tend to support this theory. Residents' perception of the quality of their housing is more positive among owners, and owners have fewer serious problems related to housing.

Whether upward mobility results in the achievement of home-ownership as status or homeownership stimulates attitudes accentuating stability and responsibility, homeowners enjoy decided financial benefits through tax advantages and capital gains and social benefits through better-maintained neighborhoods.

In theory, homeownership increases assets of homeowners through equity, increases city tax collection through property maintenance, decreases likelihood of abandonment, and aids in maintaining neighborhood stability and, therefore, maintaining property values. It is one tool for attacking an essentially economic situation. The support for this theory is considerable but it is not conclusive. Homeownership has been substantiated by several studies as a factor present in favorable urban situations. No causal relationship has been established, however.

Rehabilitation of existing housing has a similar theoretical base. It may not be a more economical method of meeting housing needs, in the long run. Rehabilitation is an intervention on the supply side of the market rather than on the demand side. Urban homesteading, homeownership through rehabilitation, is involved on both supply and demand sides of the market. It provides the supply by using existing housing. In some cases it aids with the financing for rehabilitation. This would enable the recipient to benefit from the tax advantages of homeownership as well as to support his financial outlay and risk. Although the theoretical framework tends to support the policy of urban homesteading, it is not a strong base. Whether it does alleviate these urban problems is yet to be seen.

NOTES

1. U.S. Department of Housing and Urban Development, ed., Abandoned Housing Research: A Compendium (Washington, D.C.: U.S. Government Printing Office, 1973). These figures are in the foreword and throughout the studies.

2. Ibid.

3. Ibid.

4. Michael Stegman, Housing Investment in the Inner City: The Dynamics of Decline (Cambridge, Mass.: MIT Press, 1972), p. 64.

5. James Davis, "A Second Look at the Urban Homestead," Landscape, January 1975, p. 25.

6. David Stoloff, "The National Survey of Housing Abandonment," in Abandoned Housing Research, edited by U.S. Department of Housing and Urban Development, p. 40.

7. George Sternlieb, Residential Abandonment: The Tenement Landlord Revisited (New Brunswick, N.J.: Rutgers University, 1973), p. 350.

8. Ibid., p. 29.

9. Stoloff, "The National Survey," p. 40.

10. Sternlieb, Residential Abandonment, p. 350.

11. Ibid., p. 351.

12. Stoloff, "The National Survey," p. 9.

13. Stegman, Housing Investment, pp. 96-97.

14. John D. Kasarda, "The Impact of Suburban Population Growth on Central City Service Functions," American Journal of Sociology 77, no. 6 (May 1972): 1111-24.

15. David Rasmussen, Urban Economics (New York: Harper and Row, 1973), pp. 90-91.

16. Jane Jacobs, Death and Life of Great American Cities (New York: Vintage Books, 1961). Jacobs' theories are referred to in all discussions of neighborhoods.

17. Baltimore Department of Housing and Community Development, The Settler (Baltimore, Md.: May 1975), p. 3.

18. Julia Abrahamson, A Neighborhood Finds Itself (New York: Harper and Bros.), 1959.

19. Harvey Molotch, "Racial Change in a Stable Community," American Journal of Sociology 75, no. 2 (September 1969): 226-38.

20. Linda Waller, "People Are Making It Work," Norfolk Virginian-Pilot, 26 January 1975, p. c1.

21. Raymond Rosenfeld, unpublished data collected for a study by one of the authors of Colonial Place, Norfolk, Virginia, summer 1974.

22. Martin Millspaugh and Gurney Breckenfeld, The Human Side of Urban Renewal (New York: Ives Washburn, 1960).

23. Marc Fried and Peggy Gleicher, "Some Sources of Residential Satisfaction in an Urban Slum," Journal of the American Institute of Planners 27 (November 1961): 306.

24. Jeffrey R. Solomon, "Beyond Advocacy: Toward a New Model for Community Organization," in The Mississippi Experience, edited by Paul A. Kurzman (New York: Association Press, 1971).

25. Roderick D. McKenzie, The Neighborhood: A Study of Local Life in the City of Columbus, Ohio (Chicago: University of Chicago Press, 1970).

26. James Davis, "The Urban Homestead Act," Landscape, Winter 1970, p. 13.

27. U.S. Congress, House, Committee on Banking and Currency, Subcommittee on Housing, Housing and Community Development: Hearings on H.R. 12197, 93rd Cong., 1st sess., 1973, p. 1957.

28. Frederick E. Case, Inner City Housing and Private Enterprise (New York: Praeger, 1972).

29. Douglas Committee, "Urban Housing Needs through the 1980's: An Analysis and Projection," Research Report no. 10, 1968. Prepared for the National Commission on Urban Problems.

30. Joseph Fried, "Housing for the Poor: Is it a Failure?" New York Times, 23 September 1973.

31. U.S., Statutes at Large, vol. 63, 1949. U.S. Code, vols. 12, 42, 1970.

32. Millspaugh and Breckenfeld, The Human Side, p. 223.

33. U.S., Statutes at Large, vol. 68, 1954. U.S. Code, vols. 12, 18, 20, 31, 38, 40, 42, 1970.

34. U.S., Statutes at Large, vol. 75, 1961. U.S. Code, vols. 12, 15, 40, 42, 1970.

35. U.S., Statutes at Large, vol. 78, 1965. U.S. Code, vols. 12, 20, 38, 40, 42, 1970.

36. U.S., Statutes at Large, vol. 79, 1965. U.S. Code, vols. 12, 15, 20, 38, 40, 42, 49, 1970.

37. U.S., Statutes at Large, vol. 80, 1966. U.S. Code, vol. 12, 1970.

38. Case, Inner City Housing.

39. U.S. Congress, House, Committee on Banking and Currency, Hearings on H.R. 12197, p. 1957.

40. Davis, "A Second Look," p. 24.

41. U.S. Congress, Senate, Committee on Banking, Housing and Urban Affairs, Hearings on Housing and Community Development Act: S.R. 3066, 93rd Cong., 1st sess., 1974, p. 48.

42. U.S., Statutes at Large, vol. 12, 1863.

43. George Sternlieb, The Myth and Potential Reality of Urban Homesteading (New Brunswick, N.J.: Rutgers University, Center for Urban Policy Research, 1974), p. 8.

44. Millspaugh and Breckenfeld, The Human Side, pp. 223-28.

45. Edward Freid, et. al., Setting National Priorities: The 1974 Budget (Washington, D.C.: Brookings Institution, 1973), p. 131.

46. Ibid., p. 133.

47. Michael Stegman, Housing Investment, p. 18.

CHAPTER

3

PREVIOUS WRITINGS ON HOMESTEADING

This chapter is a review of the existing literature dealing with homesteading. It is divided into three sections: 1. history and theory; 2. government participation; 3. criticism and guidelines. The literature that is cited relates only to homesteading, either rural or urban. It includes the legal precedents for homesteading, the writings that have theoretical bases in these precedents, newer theories, critiques of legal and financial problems that have been encountered or are anticipated, and various descriptive evaluations as well as some models for urban-homestead programs.

Other studies that analyze the urban problems that gave rise to urban homesteading have been discussed in Chapter 2.

HISTORY AND THEORY

Most people believe that the Rural Homestead Act[1] was the first document that enabled the government to give away land to settlers. Contrary to common belief, this was not the first such law in the United States. On August 14, 1842, Congress passed the Armed Occupation Act, "An act to provide for the armed occupation of the unsettled part of the peninsula of East Florida."[2] This act provided that any person who was head of a family or over 18 years of age, who was able to bear arms, and who would make a settlement in a certain specified area of southeast Florida would be entitled to own the land after a five-year period of residency. Eligibility was limited to those who did not own land already or who were not Florida residents. It specified that the occupant erect a house and clear and cultivate five acres of the section. It also required that the building begin within a year of occupancy.

On May 20, 1862, "An Act to Secure Homesteads to Actual Settlers on the Public Domain" was signed into law.[3] Known as the Rural Homestead Act, this law provides that any U.S. citizen or naturalized citizen over 21 who has never borne arms against the United States or given aid or comfort to its enemies is entitled to not over 160 acres of land in certain specified areas of the continental United States (west or midwest). Certain minors, under 21, who have served the army or navy in wartime for a minimum of 14 days also have the privilege of this act. The land is given free, except for a fee for the homestead application (ten dollars). The applicant signs an affidavit attesting that the application is for himself. He is required to build a structure on the land and to cultivate part of it. He must live on the land for five years. At the end of that period he must produce two witnesses to attest that he has lived on and cultivated the specified acreage for the five years immediately succeeding the filing of the affidavit.

The act further specifies that if the land is abandoned for more than six months, it reverts to the government. No lands acquired under this act become liable to satisfaction for debts incurred prior to the issuing of the "patent."

The Rural Homestead Act is still in effect. It is not used very much due to the prohibitive costs of clearing land, building roads, and so on. Since 1862, there have been 1.4 million homesteads constructed on over 247 million acres of land.[4]

A parallel act, the Morrill Act, passed in 1862, created land-grant colleges and assigned them the task of advising and counseling rural homesteaders.[5] It provided that as their primary focus, the original land-grant colleges bridge the gap between the advanced state of the agricultural art and the realities of the new homesteaders.

Many of the program elements and legal provisions of modern urban homesteading are related directly to the Rural Homestead Act. These include the eligibility requirements, the stipulation of self-occupancy, and the period of occupancy before gaining clear title. Provisions for support services can be traced to the Morrill Act. The provision that protected the rural homesteader from the loss of his property due to prior debts is presently translated into the need for financial counseling and support. Penalties that were imposed for failure to comply with the regulations are also stipulated in many urban-homestead ordinances.

Despite the earlier enactment of the Armed Occupation Act, the Rural Homestead Act remains the legal precedent most often cited as the theoretical source for urban homesteading.

One of the earliest published articles proposing urban homesteading was written by James H. Davis in 1970. Davis applied the "freeholder" theory of the Rural Homestead Act to our urban

wilderness and evolved his theory of urban homesteading from that.
His proposal stated that "People as individuals be paid with houses
and property for rebuilding those urban sections of America where
government and industry have tried to provide housing and failed."[6]

The urban homestead act that Davis proposed is based on the
theory of homeownership, to make freeholders of today's tenants.
He states that the 1862 homestead act was based on the demand for
a population of the "right sort" in a new country and that the freeholder rather than the tenant is the natural supporter of popular
government.

Davis proposed an urban homestead act coupled with a high-
technology housing system that he calls the kit (urban homestead
kit systems) system. The urban homesteading he envisioned was a
piece of real property varying in size from a plot suitable for a
single house to a share in a cooperative at greater density. The
requirements for eligibility would be limited to 21 year olds or
family heads with no restrictions for race, color, religion, sex,
education, or income. The home must meet basic living standards
within six months and must be in full compliance within two years.
(This is one form of a graduated code enforcement, the relaxing
of requirements for maintaining the housing code according to a
fixed schedule. The house generally must meet fire and safety
standards before occupancy begins; the other requirements are
staggered over a period of time to allow occupancy and rehabilitation to continue together. In some cities this requires legal changes.)
Occupancy is required for five years. The program would be conducted
on all three levels of government: homestead land would be purchased
by state government; the community would provide the physical and
social components; the housing kit, which the community would
furnish, would be paid for by the federal government; and HUD
would prepare the specifications for the kit system and select the
manufacturer. The kit system provides factory preassembled com-
ponent systems that could be assembled on-site by an unskilled
homesteader. Although Davis included the concept of rehabilitating
existing structures in his proposal, he did not amplify this suggestion.

Basing his conclusions on his evaluations of housing needs, both
quantitative and qualtative, and on the singular neglect of low-
and moderate-income groups, Davis believes that our national
housing policy is critically lacking. He supports his contention with
economic theory and cost-accounting techniques and with community
values and social techniques that would be implemented through a
community organization. As justification he discusses the feasibility
of the program on the basis of land-policy impact, market impact,
labor and industry impact, and economic impacts.

Five years later, Davis wrote "A Second Look at Urban Homesteading."[7] He found that the urban-homesteading programs of 1975
differ from his original plan because they emphasize rehabilitation
rather than new construction. His proposal was victimized, he
believed, by the monetary crunch of the 1970s. He documented the
events that gave rise to the tremendous quantity of housing abandonment. He believed large-scale abandonment was a unique event in
our history.

Davis was highly critical of urban homesteading as it has evolved.
The homesteader is a victim of the house he has inherited, Davis
asserted. "By focusing on rehabilitation, the well-off in this nation
have found another convenient way of throwing the burden back to
the poor."[8] He criticized government for not providing much help
in the form of financial aid, technical advice, or training. He called
the present versions of urban homesteading only stopgap, patched-up
versions of urban homesteading. "Only when society is willing to
finance, train and protect the new settlers of blighted areas will
urban homesteading have an effect on housing and contribute to our
social health."[9]

George Sternlieb of Rutgers University is recognized nationally
as a leading authority on urban issues, particularly housing. He
was an early proponent of urban homesteading. He based the need
on the theory of homeownership as well as on housing abandonment
and neighborhood deterioration.

A 1964 analysis that he made of tenements in Newark revealed
that homeownership was the major variable linked to housing maintenance.[10] Many students believe this study of Sternlieb's was the
basis for urban homesteading. His paper, "Toward an Urban Homestead Act," which was presented at a congressional hearing in 1971,
may have been the first formal document on the subject. In that
paper, the suggestions for homesteading are based on three theoretical assumptions: 1. that resident ownership can produce good
maintenance and good housing (homeownership); 2. that older areas
of our central cities desperately need local, responsible leadership
(neighborhood deterioration); 3. that our responsibility is to optimize
the natural movement of the market (housing economics). He defines
the areas for consideration in homesteading and presents options
within these areas: purchase price, upgrading the property, financing
the transfer, maximizing the leverage, packaging the closing, insurance, residence requirement, guidance and training. It is the area
of financing that he stresses most. He insists that the mortgage
arrangements must make market sense so that the prospective
buyer has a reasonable chance of seeing a profit from his structure.
After all the caveats are satisfied, Sternlieb projects that in homesteading we would have "a most worthwhile area."[11]

Sternlieb's most recent study of urban homesteading was presented at a conference in 1974. The Myth and Potential Reality of
Urban Homesteading questioned whether urban homesteading will
be useful in stemming the degenerative trends in urban areas or
possibly spur their reversal. Sternlieb stated that urban homesteading has not yet been properly programmed and that "its success is measured more by public relations handouts than families
housed."[12] He seemed hopeful, though, that the size of the programs
will increase sharply in the near future.

In this current study, Sternlieb analyzed homestead problems and
presented the programs he believed were essential for its success.
One basic prerogative is that the program be independent of particular personalities for its success. Another basic requirement is a
reasonable time period for a program to become operational. The
need for seeing immediate results is a deterrent to success, he said.
Sternlieb also said that urban homesteading is being misused as a
tool to save municipalities from bankruptcy.

According to Sternlieb, the program does have merit and promise,
but it needs some specific inputs: It needs revision of foreclosure
procedures; radical changes in title transfers, to give homesteaders
clear title at once; enactments to enable financing by state and local
finance agencies; changes in the mechanisms for assessing or ap-
praising; graduated levels of codes; a better takeout mechanism to
give homesteaders real financial equity; and some form of equity
insurance.

There is much pain implied in the potential of urban homesteading,
says George Sternlieb. There may be court tests of the necessary
legal enactments. The moral commitment will also involve pain and
radical change in our thinking and in our value structure.

The alarming rate in the rise of housing abandonment has been
a major factor in the development of an urban-homestead policy.
Joseph Coleman, councilman of Philadelphia, Pennsylvania, was
one of the first people to propose urban homesteading as a method
for confronting abandonment. Many other writers also address
urban homesteading on this basis.

Coleman is the person who is most often credited with first
articulating the concept of urban homesteading. In 1968, while
serving as a planning commissioner, he presented a paper to the
Philadelphia Planning Commission. His paper was titled, "Urban
Homesteading: A Plan for Developing our New Frontiers." Based
on 1960 census figures which revealed 4 million vacant but rehabilitable structures, he developed his concept of "new frontiers."[13]
In this paper he stated that vacant structures occupy a large percentage of the total city area; that these areas are economically unproductive; and that they represent our nation's new frontiers. Coleman

stressed that the life or death of this country depends upon our developing these new frontiers. Citing our previous failures to develop them, he proposed urban homesteading as a possible solution.

According to the Coleman plan, urban homesteading must involve all levels of government and also the private sector. The federal government must provide funds for clearance, provide apprentice workers to work in rehabilitation, and guarantee long-term, low-interest loans. The cities must convey title to lots and structures, grant tax exemptions, and establish a coordinating agency. Financial institutions must lend money with federal-government guarantees. Applicants must accept conditional title and contract to build or rehabilitate in a specific time frame. All these concepts are applied to the specific needs of Philadelphia. Coleman presents urban homesteading as a revolutionary concept fitting the revolutionary times in which we live.

The Wayne Law Review of March 1974 described eight methods by which housing abandonment could be attacked. One of these methods was urban homesteading. It outlined the problems and limitations of urban homesteading as they might apply to Detroit.

A HUD news release reviewed an address that HUD General Assistant Secretary Samuel C. Jackson gave before a New York State Conference of the National Association for the Advancement of Colored People in December 1972.[14] Mr. Jackson presented the homestead proposal as a realistic way to stem housing abandonment and to improve central-city neighborhoods. "Viewed in the light of its potential benefits to all society, it would be a wise investment in the social stability and quality of life in our cities," he said.[15]

Chris Drewes's in-depth study in the Columbia Journal of Law and Social Problems stated that abandonment is a critical problem and is the most urgent basis for homesteading.[16] According to his research, Drewes found that 80 percent of all housing units that were lost through abandonment in 1968 were classified as "sound" three years earlier. He suggested that city government was the logical level on which to start homesteading. He stated that the problem of the time of tax-lien foreclosure is the top-priority item for city government, because a vacant and untended building can deteriorate beyond reclamation in less than one year. He suggested a shortcut approach to defining houses as abandoned.

Mr. Drewes established his own criteria for home selection, applicant selection, program mechanics, and financing. He suggested that a pilot program should precede the full-scale implementation of homesteading. He also said that federal funding was essential, as were supplementary programs of assistance to homesteaders. All these suggestions were based on the experiences of Baltimore, Boston, Philadelphia, and Wilmington, which he documented in detail.

Though it is not simple, Mr. Drewes believes homesteading is a sound idea. He sees three concepts that need further development:

1. Abandonment—formulating a practical definition of abandoned, developing a mechanism for identifying abandoned, enabling state law to obtain quickly a clear title to properties.
2. Economics—equity of homesteader; what does he get? Condominium or co-op arrangements for larger cities.
3. Financing—adequate source of readily available capital for subsidies and low-interest loans.

GOVERNMENT PARTICIPATION

In 1976, urban homesteading was a city-initiated program. The involvement of the federal government was then pending the implementation of Section 810 of the Community Development Act. [17] State and regional levels of government had not defined their roles vis-a-vis urban homesteading.

Several writers have been concerned with government participation in the program. They discuss which level of government should initiate the program and what kind of participation should occur at every level. This debate began in the Congress. Representative Marjorie Holt (R., Md.) introduced an urban homestead bill that would have been administered by HUD as a federal program. Senator Joseph Biden (D., Del.) introduced legislation that would have been implemented on the local level. Neither bill passed. Urban homesteading remained a locally enacted and administered policy. Section 810 of the Community Development Act will provide HUD houses for local city programs. For as long as this section is in operation, the federal government will provide the housing stock, and the cities will provide all other elements of the program.

On July 11, 1973, Congresswoman Marjorie Holt addressed the House. At that time she emphasized her belief that private ownership is the key to a successful housing program. Citing the initiation of homesteading in Wilmington, Delaware, and Philadelphia, Pennsylvania, she announded that she was contacting the secretary of HUD to urge his consideration of the homesteading concept as part of a revised housing program. [18]

On September 19 of that same year, Congresswoman Holt made extended remarks to the Congress[19] regarding the need for enactment of urban homesteading on the federal level. She asserted that the recycling of abandoned dwellings was as feasible as recycling other resource materials such as scrap metal and that such a program could be cost effective.

At the same time, Ms. Holt introduced the National Homestead Act of 1973, H.S. 10373.[20] This act provided that HUD administer a homesteading program using suitable HUD-owned dwellings. It was not passed.

A similar bill, introduced by Senator Joseph Biden, met the same fate. Senator Biden's bill, S.2676, was introduced into the Senate of the United States on November 9, 1973.[21] The Biden bill provided that an urban homesteading program be administered by local agencies. The properties would be transferred to them by HUD. In his remarks on that day, Senator Biden stressed the need to cope with the "new frontiers" in cities. Urban homesteading cannot be a " cure-all," he stated, but only one of a number of undertakings that together could resolve the need for safe and decent housing in core urban areas.[22]

Public Law 93-383, an omnibus housing bill known as the Community Development Act, was signed into law on August 22, 1974. This was the first omnibus housing bill in six years—the first major housing bill in four years. The main thrust of the act is to eliminate slums and blight, conserve and expand the nation's housing stock, expand and improve community services, revitalize deteriorated neighborhoods to attract persons of higher income and restore properties for historic, architectural, or aesthetic reasons. Urban homesteading is included in Section 810 of this act. This section provides for the transfer of HUD-owned properties to local or state governments without payment, upon request. The secretary of HUD determines the suitability of these properties for homesteading based on four criteria. The act also allows the secretary of HUD to approve local homestead programs if they have certain stated provisions in their agreement with homestead families: The family must agree to occupy property for not less than three years. The family must make repairs to meet minimum health and safety standards. The family must make repairs within 18 months after occupying property. They must permit periodic inspections. The family must get "fee simple" without financial consideration. Finally, the community must have a coordinated approach toward neighborhood improvement and upgrading of community services.

Section 810 is to be funded to the extent of $5 million in 1975 and $5 million in 1976 in order to reimburse housing-loan funds for the properties transferred. The law as written seems to be unclear as to methods of how to arrive at the market value of units and, therefore, how much to reimburse insurance funds. By 1976, Section 810 had not yet been implemented.

On May 22, 1975, Carla Hills, secretary of HUD, announced that plans were being formulated for a "demonstration project" to implement Section 810 of the Community Development Act.[23] On

June 23, 1975 HUD News announced a conference to be held on
Thursday, June 26, 1975 to discuss HUD's Urban Homesteading
Demonstration Program. For purposes of discussion at that conference, HUD prepared an 11-page "Preliminary Urban Homesteading
Plan" which outlined homesteading goals as HUD interpreted them.
This document announced that the program offering of properties
would be limited to one year, 1976, and that the full funding authorization would be used for the transfer of properties. About 1,000 properties are scheduled to be transferred. The announced goals of
the demonstration are to gain insights into several aspects of
homesteading:

1. The range of property values and number of properties most
effective in improving neighborhood conditions.
2. The characteristics of neighborhoods that can be assisted with
this kind of effort.
3. The kinds of accompanying services necessary.
4. The S.E.S. (social economic status) characteristics of recip-
ients capable of becoming successful homesteaders.
5. The different administrative and financial techniques useful
in homesteading and conditions under which each of these function
best.

The program requirements for participating cities are detailed in
this publication.

Following the conference of June 26, a 38-page booklet was
written to invite participation in the demonstration, to specify conditions for participating cities, to announce selection criteria, and
to summarize the issues raised at the planning conference. Application documentation was included. According to Sybil Phillips, director of Urban Homesteading, Department of HUD, further action on
the implementation of Section 810 was delayed pending the completion
of evaluation criteria.[24]

HUD announced on October 10, 1975 that 22 cities have been
selected for an experimental program in urban homesteading.[25]
The awards were made to cities that submitted the most comprehensive plans for utilizing HUD houses in an urban-homestead program.
Whether or not federal involvement will continue beyond 1976 is
uncertain.

M. Jan Akre, a staff member of Environmental Affairs, wrote a
thorough review of the current state of urban homesteading and
presented a model for implementation in the future.[26] Ms. Akre
foresees a great value in urban homesteading. She feels that the
present programs are sufficient as pilot studies, but they need to
be reexamined for more extensive use of the program in the future.

She believes urban homesteading should be administered on a state
or regional level. Her recommendations include both administrative
and program changes.

Washington, D.C. might have had a federally administered program had home rule not intervened. In May 1974, hearings were
held before a congressional committee regarding the District of
Columbia Urban Homestead Act.[27] This bill would have established
a D.C. homestead commission, sponsored by the Congressional
Committee for Washington, D.C. If this bill had passed, the federal
government would have been involved in homesteading, insofar as its
jurisdictional supervison of Washington, D.C. is required. The bill
was not enacted. Subsequent to the adoption of home rule in Washington, the city council passed its own ordinance, which is discussed
in Chapter 5.

To date there has been little participation in urban homesteading
on the state-government level. This is probably due to the fact that
few state governments have emphasized urban problems. Only a
handful have created a department of urban affairs.

In California, pressure from citizen lobbies was brought upon
the legislature. Awareness of the impending Community Development Act provoked a number of bills in the state senate. Bill 7343
gives cities authority to operate urban homesteading programs.[28]
To date, no cities have taken advantage of this law. During the
1973-74 session of the California legislature a study of urban homesteading was requested. The study was completed on December 4,
1974. It reviews the theory and philosophy of homesteading and
describes several of the homestead programs that were in existence
at that time. The study recommends that in the event California
cities do not implement homesteading on their own, the state should
initiate the program. It suggests a property-tax exemption on repairs
and improvements for five years. It also suggests the creation of
independent city agencies or of a state agency to oversee the program
throughout the state (to provide technical advice and counseling to
homesteaders). The HUD Property Release Option Program (PROP)
program is recommended as the main source of supply for the
houses. It stresses the need for legislation to streamline foreclosure
procedures.[29] This study may encourage state participation in urban
homesteading.

Stephen C. Rother wrote a carefully documented study of urban
homesteading which was published in the January 1974 issue of New
Jersey Municipalities. It does not recommend any state-government
action. It stresses the legislation already on the state statute books
that make homesteading viable for use in New Jersy cities. Mr.
Rother recommends that the cities first contract for and supervise
all essential renovation prior to conveyance to a homesteader, then
sell the properties for the cost of renovations.[30]

CRITICISM AND GUIDELINES

Much of the literature about urban homesteading has consisted of criticism of the existing city ordinances and programs. Often these include models and guidelines for improved programs.

Mary Berry wrote one of the most comprehensive of the critiques-models articles. [31] Ms. Berry contended that homesteading was doomed to failure if it were merely a way to transfer an unpleasant burden from government agencies to homesteaders or if it were implemented on a large scale. She developed a model for demonstrating successful urban homesteading based on the following criteria:

1. Select 25 structures from the stock of abandoned houses in a contiguous neighborhood with effective heating systems, structural integrity, plumbing, and electricity.

2. Select families of all income levels. (She maintains that stipulating low income only maintains neighborhood segregation.) The main selection criteria is to be motivation and agreement to rehabilitate up to code during the five-year residency requirement. The selection priority scale was to be in the following order: a. present occupants, b. families needing relocation, c. families on public-housing waiting lists, d. families in overcrowded conditions.

3. A demonstration team should be organized to include experience in technical skills, a learning-systems person, a counselor, and a manager-bookkeeper-accountant.

Municipal Attorney, in its October 1973 issue, reviewed the basics of urban homesteading that the Housing Association of Delaware Valley had developed. After reviewing these as well as the program in Wilmington, it was concluded that urban homesteading was a boon to the cities but not to the poor. [32]

The December 1973 Architectual Forum compared the cost of rural homesteading with its urban counterpart. The relative availability and expense of materials in the city of the 1970s was contrasted with the hinterlands of a century earlier. The author expressed doubt that the program could make more than a small dent in the problem because of sheer numbers. [33]

G.U. Chamberlain, writing in American City, delineated three problems inherent in the concept of urban homesteading: getting clear title to the property; expense of rehabilitation; and state foreclosure laws. [34]

In Municipal Attorney of March 1974, Thomas Luebbers presented guidelines to strengthen the legality of homestead plans. He suggested nondiscriminatory procedures for screening applicants, acquiring

houses, and preparing for occupancy. He advocated an objective
gauge for judging the financial and mechanical qualifications of
applicants and an assurance of due process for absentee owners of
abandoned properties. [35]

Lewis B. Stone proposed a unique idea for homesteading the
cities. [36] He wants to take the apartments owned by the federal
government in public-housing projects and give them away to be
homesteaded as condominium ownerships. The economic feasibility
of this idea is developed on the basis that it would create wealth at
no one else's expense and place it in the hands of the relatively
poor. He would provide for those tenants who were financially unable
to homestead by allowing them to remain tenants of the Public
Housing Authority. Mr. Stone decries the bias that has always favored
the homeowner that allows him to deduct his real-estate tax from his
federal income tax. He stresses the economic benefits his plan creates
by being self-regulating and preserving wealth.

Beginning in the fall of 1973, various scholarly journals began to
study and review urban homesteading. The Journal of Housing featured
an article by the two executive directors of the Camden Housing
Improvements Program, D. Robinson and J.I. Weinstein. These
authors reviewed the elements of urban homesteading that Joseph
Coleman had specified earlier. Their conclusions were based on
findings in Baltimore that located 4,900 of its 5,500 vacant units
in neighborhoods of poor quality. "To give poor people a good or
fair home in a poor neighborhood may be poor planning," they concluded. [37]

The Fordham Urban Law Journal presented a strong case for
urban homesteading with certain specified caveats. [38] It hypothesized
that urban homesteading is best used as a specialized tool for improving
neighborhoods in smaller cities and that it will be more likely to
succeed if it can attract middle- and upper-class families. Although
the primary motivation is neighborhood rehabilitation rather than
family rehabilitation, the effect is the same. An analysis of Wilmington and Philadelphia on the basis of these hypotheses finds that
Wilmington has more advantages for success.

A landmark ruling in the case of Love v. Hoffman of Dallas
County, Texas, was handed down by the Supreme Court in 1973. [39]
This ruling established a formula for tax exemptions.

A rash of news and feature stories appeared in the press and
popular magazines following the announcement of Wilmington's first
lottery to select homesteaders and the subsequent announcements
from other cities of their plans for homesteading. The first major
coverage of the event appeared in the New York Times on September 16, 1973. [40] A story in the Wall Street Journal followed on
September 21, 1973. [41] Benjamin Ronis, well-known Washington

architect and planner, wrote a lengthy critique in the Washington
Post on September 22, 1973. There were many others. All were
datelined Wilmington, Delaware, and all presented some aspects
of the Wilmington program. Mr. Ronis stood almost alone among
the columnists in his skepticism. He compared the modern homesteader to the nineteenth-century one and found there was little
similarity. Rural homesteaders worked on their homes and their
land as their full-time occupation. They had a choice of desirable
homesites. Urban homesteaders must take over the dregs of the
nation's housing inventory, earn their livelihood away from home,
and find additional time and energy to restore abandoned dwellings.
Then, having done this, the value of the home is still uncertain, for
today's real-estate values are based on location more than size
or quality. Mr. Ronis believes that we need a change in property-
tax laws. The tax laws are as much to blame in the creation of
urban blight as some of the more apparent factors, he says. [42]

U.S. News and World Report reviewed homestead plans and
progress in Wilmington, Washington, Baltimore, and Philadelphia.
It pointed out various problems such as foreclosure procedures,
inner-city employment, and declining real-estate values. [43]

All the cities that initiated homesteading had full coverage in
their local press. Many of these articles were picked up by the
Associated Press and reprinted in papers all over the United States.
Two such articles were reprinted in the Tidewater, Virginia, papers. [44]
Each reviewed the current scope and some of the literature of home-
steading.

Savings and Loan News, in a lengthy story, emphasized the
economic determinants of a successful homesteading effort. [45]
Family Circle featured pictures of homesteads before and after
rehabilitation. [46]

On May 30, 1975, Wayne King wrote his second story on homesteading for the New York Times. [47] This time around, King's
initial enthusiasm for homesteading had turned to disappointment.
"Urban Homestead Faltering," the headline says. King focused on
Baltimore and described various failures. He highlighted the security
problems.

Two case studies provided thorough and in-depth materials and
details on policies, goals, and programs of the first four cities
to enact urban homesteading. Urban Homesteading: Process and
Potential resulted from a workshop conducted by the National Urban
Coalition. [48] HUD's Neighborhood Preservation is a catalog which
includes a section on the cities that have urban-homestead programs. [49]
The legal and financial aspects of each of four city programs are
described. Detailed analysis of the programs is included.

All the documents, studies, and stories described here have
provided the authors with background for a better understanding

of the cities we observed and of the documents and materials that we received.

NOTES

1. U.S., Statutes at Large, vol. 12, 1863.

2. U.S., Statutes at Large, vol. 5, 1856.

3. Ibid.

4. U.S. Department of Interior, Bureau of Land Management, Homesteading, Past and Present (December 1963), p. 3.

5. Statutes at Large, vol. 12, 1862.

6. James Davis, "The Urban Homestead Act," Landscape, Winter 1970, p. 14.

7. James Davis, "A Second Look at Urban Homesteading," Landscape, January 1975, pp. 23-27.

8. Ibid., p. 26.

9. Ibid.

10. George Sternlieb, Residential Abandonment: The Tenement Landlord Revisited (New Brunswick, N.J.: Rutgers University, Center for Urban Policy Research, 1973).

11. George Sternlieb, "Toward an Urban Homestead Act," in Hearings of the Committee on Banking and Currency (Washington, D.C.: U.S. Government Printing Office, 1971).

12. George Sternlieb, The Myth and Potential Reality of Urban Homesteading (New Brunswick, N.J.: Rutgers University, Center for Urban Policy Research, 1974), p. 1.

13. Joseph E. Coleman, Esq., "Urban Homesteading: A Plan for Developing Our New Frontiers," paper presented to the Philadelphia Planning Commission, 1968.

14. U.S. Department of Housing and Urban Development, "'Homesteading' in Cities Suggested by HUD Official," HUD News, 21 October 1972.

15. Ibid., p. 2.

16. Chris W. Drewes, "Homesteading 1974: Reclaiming Abandoned Houses on the Urban Frontier," Columbia Journal of Law and Social Problems 10 (Spring 1974): 416-55.

17. U.S. Congress, House, Housing and Community Development Act of 1974, 93rd Cong., 1974, p. 101.

18. U.S. Congress, House, Congressional Record, 93rd Cong., 1st sess., 1973, 119, p. H 5935. Congresswoman Holt speaking for urban homesteading, 11 July 1973.

19. U.S. Congress, House, Congressional Record, 93rd Cong., 1st sess., 1973, 119, p. E5888. Congresswoman Holt speaking on federal housing programs, 19 September 1973.

20. Ibid.

21. U.S. Congress, Senate, Congressional Record, 93rd Cong., 1st sess., 1973, 119, part 28, pp. 36487-88. Senator Biden speaking for the Urban Homestead Act.

22. Ibid.

23. Marjorie Holt, Congresswoman, news release, 22 May 1975.

24. Sybil Phillips, letter to the authors, 22 August 1975.

25. U.S. Department of Housing and Urban Development, HUD News, 10 October 1975.

26. M. Jan Akre, "Urban Homesteading: Once More Down the Yellow Brick Road," Environmental Affairs 3, no. 3 (1974): 563-94.

27. U.S. Congress, House, Committee on the District of Columbia, Subcommittee on the Judiciary. Urban Homesteading: Hearings on H.R. 12197, 93rd Cong., 2nd sess., 1974. pp. 1-106.

28. California Senate, Committee on Government Organization, Urban Homesteading: Sweat Equity at Work Helping to Solve the Housing Problems, mimeographed (Sacramento, Calif.: 4 December 1974), p. 40.

29. Ibid., pp. 43-45.

30. Steven C. Rother, "Urban Homesteading: It May be One Way to Reclaim Abandoned City Dwellings," New Jersey Municipalities, January 1974, p. 14.

31. Mary Berry, "Homesteading New Prescription for Urban Ills," HUD Challenge, January 1974. pp. 2-5.

32. "Urban Homesteading," Municipal Attorney 14, no. 10 (October 1973): 196, 216.

33. "Urban Homesteading," Architectural Forum 139 (December 1973): 75.

34. G.U. Chamberlain, "Homesteading Offers Antidote for Urban Blight," American City 89 (January 1974): 60.

35. Thomas A. Luebbers, "Guidelines for Urban Homesteading," Municipal Attorney 15, no. 3 (March 1974): 75, 95.

36. Lewis B. Stone, "An Urban Homestead Act," Current, March 1973, pp. 3-5.

37. D. Robinson and J.E. Weinstein, "Urban Homesteading: Hope. . .or Hoax," Journal of Housing (August- September 1973): 395.

38. "From Plows to Pliers: Urban Homesteading in America," The Fordham Urban Law Journal 2 (Winter 1974): 273-304.

39. Love v. Hoffman, 499 SW2d 295 (1973).

40. Joseph P. Fried, "Housing for Poor: Is it a Failure?" New York Times, 16 September 1973.

41. Gail Bronson, "The Old Homestead," Wall Street Journal, 21 September 1973.

42. Benjamin Ronis, "A Wilmington Experiment," Washington Post, 22 September 1973.

43. "Homesteading in 1973—City Houses for $1," U.S. News and World Report, 5 November 1973, p. 44.

44. Thomas Lippman, "The Urban Homestead—A New Kind of Frontier," Norfolk Virginian-Pilot, 17 February 1974; Wilfred Owen, "Planned Cities Make 'Downtown' Nice Place to Live," Norfolk Virginian-Pilot, 14 March 1975, p. D 15.

45. "Urban Homesteading—Saving Old Housing is the Name of the Claim," Savings and Loan News, M 95 (January 1974): 50-54.

46. Jean Anderson, "You Can Buy a House for $1—Yes, $1," Family Circle, April 1975, pp. 90-91, 128, 130.

47. Wayne King, "Urban Homesteading Faltering in Fight against Blight of Cities," New York Times, 30 May 1975, p. C 1.

48. National Urban Coalition, Urban Homesteading: Process and Potential (Washington, D.C.: National Urban Coalition, January 1974).

49. U.S. Department of Housing and Urban Development, Office of Policy Development and Research, Neighborhood Preservation: A Catalog of Local Programs (Washington, D.C.: U.S. Government Printing Office, February 1975).

4

RESEARCH METHODS
AND PROCEDURES

The goal of this study is to describe and analyze urban home-steading as it existed in the summer of 1975. The nature of the problem created certain limitations to the usual scientific research. As new local public policies, these programs are still developing and adapting to each city's environment. Each city has a concern for the privacy rights of its clients, making the fieldwork difficult to accomplish.

DEFINING THE UNIVERSE

The first priority was to determine the universe. There has been no comprehensive work written on urban homesteading and no compilation of cities implementing the policy. In order to locate literature related to the policy and to locate the programs, letters were sent to urban institutes and authorities. These were selected according to their proximity to an existing program known to the authors, because they were in a city known to have a large stock of abandoned housing, or because of a specialized interest in urban-housing problems exhibited by the organization. Queries also were made of other specialists in the field of housing policy, legislators representing Tidewater, Virginia on all levels of government, and people named in articles on homesteading. From these replies a list was made of cities that either had a homesteading program or had expressed an interest in the concept. Letters were sent to these 29 cities requesting any information on the program or status of the development of a program. Replies were received from 23 cities. From all these sources, the universe of urban-homesteading programs was determined.

The definition of urban homesteading varied widely. The authors had originally intended to study one type, known to exist in only three cities: Houses were given to citizens for one dollar with the promise to rehabilitate and occupy them for several years. As we discovered the scope of interest that the policy has generated and the variations in implementation, we decided to expand the definition to include all programs called urban homesteading. It was thought that in the realm of public policy, the name itself had an impact on the public image of the program. Therefore, all should be studied as representative of the program. Since the number of cities that were interested in urban homesteading was changing each month, a status file was created. Those operating the program through the spring and summer of 1975 were included in the survey study for more detailed descriptions.

A survey of 11 cities with operating programs was planned for an in-depth description of their policies. New York City and Dayton were to be described from published material gained elsewhere. Since they were not known to be homesteading cities at the time of the design, it was considered that the total universe would be in the study. More letters were sent to these 11 cities requesting specific information in order to determine the types of data needed from the survey. We requested the titles of all officials and administrators involved in the program, a copy of the ordinance, a copy of the financial forms used for application to become homesteaders, evaluation forms, goal statements, and any other information that the city thought would be helpful. (Confidentiality by the authors was stressed, of course.) Four of the cities (Baltimore, Wilmington, St. Louis, and Minneapolis) responded with widely differing materials, much of it beyond our requests. This material was used in the development of the hypotheses for the survey.

HYPOTHESES

The hypotheses were centered on the specific program elements and their impact on the client group and on the wider community. They addressed the following problems:

1. Does the community at large support the concept of homesteading?

2. Does the community feel that homesteading will improve the city? If so, how?

3. Has business been affected by homesteading? If so, how has it been affected?

4. Does the type of administration affect the homesteading program?

5. What are the problems and how do they affect the program?

6. Are there uses for abandoned single-family dwellings other than homesteading?

7. What socioeconomic groups benefit directly from urban homesteading?

8. Does homesteading make homeownership available to people who could not otherwise own homes?

9. Does the income level of the homesteader affect the type of problems encountered in homesteading?

10. Are homesteaders discouraged by the program-related problems?

11. Does homesteading improve the vitality of neighborhoods?

12. How does homesteading really work? (Investigation into this problem resulted in the case studies.)

The other problems were formed into the following hypotheses for an analysis of each group affected by homesteading.

1. If urban homesteading exists in a city, civic leaders will respond to its presence.

2. If urban homesteading exists in a city, then civic leaders perceive improvements.

3. If urban homesteading exists in a city, civic leaders observe a change in business activity.

4. If there is a difference in administrative structure in cities with similar numbers of available houses, the programs will differ.

5. If there is a difference in the size of the urban-homesteading program, then the problems encountered will differ.

6. In the opinion of urban-homestead officials, there are possible adaptations of the single-family-dwelling program.

7. Homesteaders represent a homogeneous socioeconomic group.

8. If urban homesteading exists, certain citizens have the opportunity for homeownership.

9. If homesteaders are in a certain income group, this will be reflected in their racial characteristics and the homesteading problems they encounter.

10. If certain homesteading problems and finance methods exist, then homesteader satisfaction is affected.

11. If homesteading is present, homesteaders perceive a change in neighborhood stability.

SCHEDULES AND POPULATIONS

In order to test these hypotheses, three sets of populations were chosen for the study: homesteading officials, homesteaders who have lived in their "new" home for a period of time, and civic leaders. The three questionnaire surveys sent to them were based on the following three premises: (1) the success of urban homesteading is related to civic leaders' perceptions about the program; (2) the success of urban homesteading is related to officials' views and attitudes; (3) the success of urban homesteading is related to homesteaders' satisfaction. Separate schedules were designed for each group. (See Appendix B.)

The civic leaders' schedule was designed to learn of possible community impact of the policy. (See Appendix B.) The questions related to business impact, community opposition, and possible effects on the neighborhoods, the city budget, and the community. Civic leaders, it was hypothesized, would not be as bound by political decisions or administrative structure in their response to the program as the officials. Two groups were chosen to represent the community pulse: the chamber of commerce and the board of realtors. These organizations seemed the closest to community opinion and to knowledge of current, city housing programs. The survey included one chamber of commerce official and one representative of the board of realtors. The chamber of commerce was chosen because this group is usually composed of people who are both visible and audible in the community, who are concerned about the social and economic problems of a city, and who express these concerns to the elected officials with some degree of effectiveness. Chamber of commerce directors, it was thought, would be sensitive to an urban-homesteading program in terms of how it would affect the economic and social life of the community. Additionally, we assumed that their opinions concerning the future of urban homesteading would be made known and would carry considerable weight with decision makers. Finally, one of the authors, Zelma Rivin, is a board director of the Portsmouth, Virginia chamber of commerce. From this experience, we knew of chamber interest in local-government programs and their effect on the city.

The board of realtors was selected because of their obvious sensitivity to a program affecting housing. It seemed this would be the first group that would be aware of any changes in the housing

market that could be related to homesteading. Since homesteading
has been initiated as a pilot program in most cities and since the
program takes several years to become effective in the marketplace,
many civic leaders might not at this point be aware of the program
or sensitive to its impact. However, we believed that any slight
change would be noticed by realtors and chamber of commerce
directors.

The officials' questionnaire schedule was designed to give facts
on the program as well as some opinion on the success of the program. Officials of the homestead staff were the target group. We
were interested in the officials' opinions regarding homesteading
in areas other than single-family dwellings as well as present
program implementation. As agents of the policy, they would be
the most closely associated with the program. Since the facts requested made the schedule lengthy, only one such schedule of facts
and opinions was sent to each city. Three forms of the opinion
schedule were sent to each city. The long schedule, which included
both fact and opinion questions, was the most successful. Since the
shorter forms were not always distributed either because of a
small staff or a lack of time, the few returns were dropped from
further consideration in the study.

The homesteaders' questionnaire schedule included demographic
facts, attitudes toward program elements, and attitudes toward the
neighborhood. (See Appendix B.) It was designed for those homesteaders who had lived in their new location long enough to be able
to describe it in relation to their former home. This does not include
all the homesteaders at the time of the study since some were in the
initial acquisition or rehabilitation stages and not yet occupying the
homestead. In some cities the authors did not know the number of
homesteaders in the program. A level of ten was established for each
city, initially. These ten forms were sent to the local office of urban
homesteading. A cover letter described the appropriate population
for whom the questionnaire was designed.

Pretests of the homesteaders' and officials' schedules were
carried out in a graduate sociology class, using students who had
heard of the program and could imagine the answers. The students
had also studied administrative structures of several public services.
The class discussion of the questionnaires after they had been administered produced criticisms that were helpful in the redesigning of
certain questions. The officials' schedule was given to a local administrator of a similar program to determine the ease and time of
self-administration as well as content relevancy for administrators.
The limitations of these schedules revolved around the type of data
requested, factual and attitudinal on experiences of varying intensity.
Hence, the data gathered was initially analyzed as nominal-level
data.

The validity of the study is difficult to measure since no comparable study has been published. In-house publications received from the cities, however, tend to establish these questions as being of wide interest. Almost the exact same data was sought for annual reports in Baltimore, Minneapolis, Philadelphia, Rockford, and Wilmington. The attitudes and impacts, beyond homesteader socioeconomic status, were not reported in any of the literature. This study is the first to consider these aspects of homesteading. All the cities expressed an interest in the data from this study. The design of an urban-homesteading evaluation proposal presently under consideration by HUD contains the same objective as those addressed in our schedules, with the exception of community impact. Our attempt to measure this area remains unique. The interest of these other sources tends to establish the validity of the schedules as designed. It is the only study of such scope. Most of the cities have not been reported in any published studies.

The total population of the officials was included, and the total population of homesteaders occupying their new home was included (except in the cities of Newark and St. Louis where 300 homesteaders each were involved). A director of each of the two community groups most closely related to community pulse and knowledge of city housing programs was included. Therefore, the choice of interviewees seems valid.

The scope of cities included in the study and the scope of affected groups interviewed are the two factors that make this study especially unique. It also makes it useful for future research into the impact of urban homesteading on urban problems. This study essentially breaks new ground in urban-homesteading research.

SURVEY

Realizing the importance of the study and the need to have some on-site interviews and inspections, the authors sought and received a grant from the Graduate Studies Department at Old Dominion University, Norfolk, Virginia. This grant of $248.00 made a field trip possible, which proved to be invaluable in understanding the program.

The actual surveying was conducted in two phases. First, a field trip was made to Washington, D.C.; Wilmington, Delaware; and Baltimore, Maryland. Second, the mail questionnaire forms were sent to the other eight cities. The field trip was designed to validate the hypotheses as well as to observe the operation of the program and the houses in the program. It also gave us the opportunity to administer the questionnaires. Another purpose was to photograph the homes for a more graphic presentation of the descriptions of the cities.

A trip was made to Washington, Wilmington, and Baltimore from June 2 to June 5, 1975. It was beneficial to our understanding of the environmental differences creating varying programs. We discovered through correspondence and through the on-site visits that personal contact with the homesteaders would be impossible because of privacy rights. At that point it was decided that all questionnaires would be mailed, except to the officials seen on the field trip. These were interviewed in person with later additions made by mail, completing the facts on the program. The houses were visited and photographed. This aided in the descriptions of house deterioration possible for homesteading, of varying sources of houses in the different cities, and of homestead-neighborhood appearances.

The validity of the mail versus the interview questionnaire was minimized with the elite population used. The 11 officials were asked technical questions unanswerable by any other group. A study of the problem of mail versus interview techniques was conducted with the Georgia State Legislature, and the results showed very slight differences in the two groups.[1] The mail group tended to have more "don't know" answers—a difference in intensity. There were no substantial differences in the responses as to content.

The homesteaders' and officials' questionnaire forms were mailed to the urban-homesteading office in each city. The director was requested to mail the homesteader forms to the homesteaders occupying their new homes. Return envelopes for all were provided. The civic-leader questionnaire forms were mailed to their respective organizations for delivery to a board member.

The follow-up had two phases. Telephone calls were placed to the program directors for the officials' questionnaire forms, and letters were sent to the homesteaders. Follow-up letters on chamber of commerce stationery from the Portsmouth Chamber of Commerce executive secretary were sent to the civic leaders. The follow-up on homesteaders was especially difficult since it depended on an indirect request. The letters again were sent to the director for distribution. Telephone calls were very useful in raising the rate of return of both sets of questionnaires. They also helped keep the authors current on the number in the program. Since there was no record of who the homesteaders were that we were reaching, the reliability of returns is difficult to establish. Most of the programs are very small, however, and there was a high rate of return (see Table 4.1). By the answers it was obvious whether or not the respondents had begun to occupy their homestead sites.

The only problems encountered were in Philadelphia, Newark, and St. Louis. Philadelphia did not distribute the forms to the homesteaders because of another study being conducted in that city. A Newark official stated that there were "around 300" in the program;

TABLE 4.1

Questionnaire Returns*

	Civic Leader		Official		Homesteader		Total
	Sent	Returned	Sent	Returned	Sent	Returned	Received
Baltimore	2	1	1	1	30	16 (53%)	18
Buffalo	2	1	1	0	0	0 (0%)	2
Camden	2	1	1	0	5	2 (40%)	3
Minneapolis	2	1	1	1	4	2 (50%)	4
Newark	2	2	1	0	10	0 (0%)	2
Philadelphia	2	1	1	1	35	0 (0%)	2
Pittsburgh	2	0	1	1	48	2 (4%)	3
Rockford	2	2	1	0	22	4 (18%)	6
St. Louis	2	2	1	1	70	25 (36%)	28
Washington	2	2	1	1	12	5 (42%)	8
Wilmington	2	1	1	1	5	4 (80%)	6
Total	22	14 (64%)	11	7 (64%)	241	60 (25%)	82

*The total homesteader returns are a low percentage, mainly because of the lack of deliveries in Newark and Philadelphia. The percentage of the total delivered that were returned was 31%.

Source: Compiled by the authors.

43

however, the ten questionnaire forms were mislaid and never completed and returned. St. Louis also had about 300 homesteaders
who were in their homes. Seventy questionnaire forms were sent,
the limit that the study budget would allow. One respondent stated
that he was not yet in his house because it was occupied and that he
needed legal help in getting the occupants out. Otherwise, the returns
seemed to be reliable representations of the facts and attitudes of
the population sought.

Since the study was attempting to describe the total population,
the level of confidence was not considered in the analysis of the
data. It was a factor in the number of returns, however. Of the 11
officials' questionnaire forms sent, 8 were completed and returned.
Of the 241 homesteaders' questionnaire forms sent, 196 seem to
have been delivered by the urban-homesteading offices. There were
62 returned, of which 60 were completed. Twenty-two civic leaders'
questionnaire forms were sent, 11 to the chambers of commerce and
11 to the boards of realty. There were 14 completed and returned.

The indirect process of sending the homesteader questionnaire
forms slowed the returns. Because of completion deadlines, the
coding was done with a limited number of returns. Twin problems
of a small population and a wide variety in responses led to a decision to collapse categories as much as possible, according to data
received. Later returns were sometimes difficult to fit into the
categories established. These were adjusted to accommodate the
new data as much as possible, but sometimes new categories had
to be created. The result was a lowering of the level of significance
among the cross tabulations in many instances. The statistical
methods used were cross tabulations and variable totals. Percentages were used when appropriate. These were the most useful in
meeting the goal of providing a description of urban homesteading.

There is the possibility of converting the data for use in a
multiple regression or factorial analysis to determine common
elements or influences in the program. This could be done as a
replication of Sternlieb's tenement-landlord study to test his neighborhood stability conclusions. However, it was decided that time
and the size of the program were not sufficient to warrant such an
analysis at present.

PRESENTATION OF DATA

There were two techniques employed for data analysis: descriptive case studies of the cities and statistical analyses of the three
affected groups. The case studies were necessary in order to obtain
and present base data on the cities. Because little research has been

done on urban homesteading, descriptive work is appropriate. These in-depth descriptions are unique to the literature of urban home-steading. They provide an opportunity for comparison or modeling in future research. They also provide clear pictures of homesteading in 11 different settings.

Each city is presented separately in Chapter 5. Each case study is divided into sections concerning the background of the program and its unique characteristics (the environment), the laws and administration (the policy), the support services (the implementa-tion), and the benefits (the impact). These sections are the elements needed for future evaluation. The findings are described in the series of comparative tables that conclude the chapter. Data from the case studies were used in developing the statistical-analysis portion of this study.

One of the purposes of this research was to determine the impact of the program within each city. The perceptions of the affected groups are the measures of impact that were used. Producer per-ceptions and consumer perceptions were measured by means of the questionnaire surveys of the officials (producers of the program) and the homesteaders (consumers of the program's benefits). Other benefits, or externalities, may be found elsewhere in the community. These were measured by the surveys of citizen satisfaction with the program. The civic leaders represent the citizen group.

This extra dimension of impact offered a more comprehensive understanding of the program. The output (number of homestead sites) did not reflect by itself whether or not homesteading was reaching its goals. The statistical analyses by the affected groups offers an additional insight into the effects of the program. This was not obtainable from the aggregate data or program facts that were used in the case studies.

These two techniques, descriptive and statistical analyses, were especially appropriate at this point in the history of urban home-steading. The size of the programs was appropriate for study, as well as their local similarities and differences. They provided the necessary types of analyses for fulfilling the purposes of this work.

NOTE

1. Frank K. Gibson and Brett W. Hawkins, "Interviews versus Questionnaires," American Behavioral Scientist 12 (September-October 1968): NS9-16.

CHAPTER

5

CASE STUDY ANALYSIS
OF HOMESTEADING
IN 11 CITIES

All previous studies of any type on urban homesteading concentrate on the two or three first programs, at most. Our goal was to study the total population of cities with homestead programs. The preliminary research revealed that as of June 1975, there were 13 such cities. We were able to gather data about 11 of these for in-depth case studies: Baltimore, Maryland; Buffalo, New York; Camden, New Jersey; Minneapolis, Minnesota; Newark, New Jersey; Philadelphia, Pennsylvania; Pittsburgh, Pennsylvania; Rockford, Illinois St. Louis, Missouri; Washington, D.C.; and Wilmington, Delaware. Sufficient information on Dayton, Ohio and New York City was not available. New York's Urban Homesteading Assistance Board (U-HAB) program was described to a limited degree in Neighborhood Preservation: A Catalog of Local Programs.[1] This will be discussed in Chapter 7 under the possible future implications.

The original three—Baltimore, Wilmington, and Philadelphia— were included because different data were sought. These cities, although often studied, had not been compared to the other, newer programs. Questionnaire schedules were used to gather the data from the three groups affected within each city. This included the homesteaders, homestead officials, and civic leaders. They furnished a base of comparable data between cities. Other data sources included in-house reports, outside studies, and the Census Bureau. These three cities are similar in several respects. All are old, eastern cities with a large stock of old brick housing.

The same research methods were used for the rest of the cities. Some cities were able to provide more data than others; hence, more detailed case studies were written for some. The information was organized to cover environmental factors, program elements,

and citizen opinions. These three elements were described in the
following form:

- Background
- Unique characteristics
- Legislation and administration
- Financial options
- Support services
- Benefits as perceived by officials, civic leaders, and home-
  steaders

Following each city case study is a table covering pertinent
census data and comparable figures, where applicable, from homestead data. After this are tables describing the administration path
and the homesteader path from inception to completion of the program. The conclusion to this section is a series of comparative
tables on the programs of the various cities.

The on-site inspection of the three cities of Washington, Wilmington, and Baltimore was helpful in clarifying our understanding
of the administration and implementation differences. This insight
helped us interpret with more understanding the data from the
cities not visited. In addition, these three case studies include personal observations not possible elsewhere.

The 11 cities will be introduced in alphabetical order.

BALTIMORE, MARYLAND

Baltimore was one of the three cities visited by the authors in
June 1975. It was chosen because of its large and varied program.
Due to the great effort and time that Mr. Roger Windsor, Home
Ownership Development Program director, spent with us, we were
able to view all the homestead programs as well as several other
related home-ownership programs in the city of Baltimore.

Background

The goal of Baltimore's homestead program addresses two major
problems that the city defined: a large number of abandoned houses
and a decline in the homeownership rate. In 1970, Baltimore began
to note a drop in homeownership; for the first time in 30 years the
city had fewer owners than renters. The Home Ownership Development Program (HODP) was the response to this problem—an attempt
to revitalize and stabilize the decline in homeownership. In July 1973,

HODP began to implement homesteading as one aspect of its program. There are 5,458 abandoned houses in Baltimore. The city owns 2,705 of these. Of these properties, 1,184 have been recommended for homesteading. In stating its goal, the Baltimore homestead program cites the problems: "To return vacant and neglected houses to the housing inventory, to promote their rehabilitation, and to spur home ownership."[2]

Baltimore utilizes two concepts in its homestead program: scattered-site rehabilitation and clustered or concentrated rehabilitation. Most of the houses are in scattered sites. These properties came to city ownership by way of tax delinquency. The clustered properties on Stirling Street were acquired under urban-renewal powers.

In all, the present program consists of 105 houses. Twenty-five of these are clustered on Stirling Street. The remaining 80 are scattered throughout the city. Thirty-five of these were totally rehabilitated and occupied as of June 1975. It seems necessary to point out that the Stirling Street sites, which were scheduled for demolition, were in extreme states of dilapidation. In many instances the roofs, sidewalls, and even the flooring were beyond repair. Additionally, the houses were very small; some were only two-room structures. Several homesteaders have combined two of these to create multiple-room dwellings. This is in contrast to the average homestead property which is a two- or three-story brick structure.

Baltimore is experimenting with "shopsteading," that is, allowing homesteaders to rehabilitate shopfront properties. When this type of homesteading is used, only the residential portion of the property is eligible for a Residential Environmental Assistance Loan (REAL), the city loan. At the present time, the building of new structures on vacant land is not incorporated into the program.

Thirty interview forms for homesteaders were left in Baltimore on June 6, 1975 when the authors conducted on-site inspections in that city. Sixteen have been returned. In addition, two official forms and one civil-leader form were returned.

Unique Characteristics

A combination of environmental factors and administrative structure enhance Baltimore's homestead program. The geography and history comprise one unique feature. Baltimore, one of the oldest cities in the United States, has many areas where architectural style, street design, and building materials make restoration both desirable and appealing. Historical restoration is a major activity throughout the city. A recognition of the historic value of some of the deteriorated houses and abandoned neighborhoods has led to renewed interest in conservation of these sites, especially when they have been designated homestead areas. Stirling Street is one such section. Originally scheduled for demolition, its potential was recognized, and the small row houses on an irregular hill were offered for homesteading. The success of this project is a highlight of Baltimore's program. Ridgely's Delight offers homesteaders the opportunity to live in an area recorded in Baltimore's history as early as 1668.[3] Otterbein, a new homestead offering in Baltimore, provides an appeal similar to Stirling Street. Its focal point is a historic church; and the area is bordered by a redevelopment area scheduled to contain a variety of dwelling units.

The Baltimore HODP supervises all homeownership-related activities in the city, including inspection-code enforcement, redevelopment, financing, and other services. This curtails much red tape that normally prevails in homesteading programs. The homesteader accomplishes all his needs through one office, the Department of Housing and Community Development (DHCD), and the homestead program can expedite its work. The city-funded loans simplify the financial procedure for the homesteader. His qualification as a homesteader also certifies him for the REAL loans. This loan program is funded from a $2 million bond issue which provides rehabilitation funds at 6-percent interest.

Another unique characteristic is the city's Vacant Property Monitoring System. It facilitates up-to-date identification of potential properties for homesteading.

Laws and Administration

Because Baltimore is an independent body of the commonwealth, the city did not need extensive legal enactments to inaugurate its homestead program. The original resolution was adopted by the Board of Estimates in 1973. Baltimore's independent status also enabled it to act with haste on the matter of property acquisition. According to the Annotated Code of Maryland, Article 81, Section 100, the city may gain title to a property six months after a tax sale or within two months if the property is in need of substantial repair.[4]

There is no homestead board. The director of HODP administers a staff of seven. Three of these are involved in the early phases of the program: selecting, marketing, and counseling. Four work in the award-to-completion phase as cost estimators, bid-contract executors, and inspectors. The total cost of this administration is $120,000 annually, or $1,000 per unit.[5]

The house selection is based on the condition of the blocks where they are located. Two types of blocks have been used. In one type only a few houses are deteriorated. In the other, all the houses on the block need rehabilitation and the entire block is worth restoring. An effort is made to offer houses in areas where other community-development programs are in operation. This enables homeowners to reinforce each other. There is no conflict between programs since they are all administered by the same staff. Individual houses are inspected by DHCD to determine structural and economic feasibility for rehabilitation to code standards.

The major criteria for homesteaders are financial ability and need for housing. Additional considerations are credit rating, dependents, and how much the individual can reduce the cost of rehabilitation by contributing to the actual work (knowledge of building skills). Preference is given to renters, and some effort is made to match household size to homestead size. Applicants must be 18 years or older and U.S. citizens or registered aliens. Single men and women are considered households and are therefore eligible for the program. No lottery has been used. To date only one applicant has been qualified for each homestead.

Marketing and publicizing is done in three ways: through The Settler, an in-house publication of DHCD which features one or two homestead parcels each month as well as other information regarding homesteading; through advertisements in four local newpapers; through open houses. Revolving lists of potential homesteads are always available from the Home Ownership Development Program on request.

Financial Options

Homesteaders may borrow money from the REAL loan fund. The financial limit on REAL loans is $17,400; interest is 6-percent for a term of 20 years. If the property is located in an active federally assisted area, Section 312 loans are available at 3 percent. This enabled the Stirling Street homesteaders to use both 312 and REAL loans.

Most homesteaders sign a lease-purchase agreement with the city. They do not receive clear title until rehabilitation is complete. In those cases, Baltimore is the title holder and HODP contracts for the rehabilitation work, with approval of the homesteader. The REAL staff holds the rehabilitation loan money in escrow until the contracted work has been certified. Since these homesteaders do not actually own the property, they pay no property taxes for the two-year rehabilitation period. In essence the city foregoes property taxes on most homesteads for two years.

In order to qualify for a Section 312 loan, an applicant must take title to the property before the loan is approved. In those cases applicants must pay property taxes.

Support Services

Homesteaders receive special services both during the period of application and the period of actual homesteading. The applicant is provided with a detailed cost estimate and priority work schedule. Financial counseling and help with loan applications are also provided to the applicant. As a homesteader, one is helped in every aspect of the rehabilitation: choosing and qualifying contractors; inspecting and certifying the contracted work; counseling when contractors do not meet commitments or present other problems. A guide, Home Rehabilitation: How to Start It, How to Finish It, How to Manage It, is given to every homesteader. Rehabilitation workships are held periodically by interested citizens' groups. Community organizations are encouraged and counseled. The building code is relaxed for the first two years. The applicant may occupy the homestead as soon as the fire and safety regulations are satisfied. Other building-code requirements are fulfilled during occupancy and must be completed within two years of the signing of the agreement. Volunteer services in the fields of architecture and planning are provided by the Neighborhood Design Center.

Benefits to City

The questionnaires that were returned from homesteaders and the HODP officials in Baltimore all indicated great satisfaction with the program. Roger Windsor, director of HODP, calls homesteading "the hottest program in town." He stresses the racial and economic integration it is fostering. He credits homesteading with creating a "real revitalization of interest in the city. . .it places the whole perspective of the city in a different light."[6]
"A Cost-Benefit Analysis of the Baltimore Urban Scattered-Site Homestead Program" lists many benefits to the city:

1. Home ownership—community stability.
2. Quick process of converting from sub-standard to adequate.
3. Other home owners improve their properties—community spirit in neighborhood.
4. Houses back on the tax rolls in 18 months.

5. Provides housing for moderate income in downtown—
   bringing people back into city (additional revenue)—
   reverses white flight.
6. Lessening of maintenance and demolition costs—
   reduction in police and fire calls.
7. Retain houses of historical significance.[7]

Another Baltimore official notes a marked increase in city morale:
"The enthusiasm of homesteaders causes other city residents to
reevaluate their feelings toward the city's revitalization."

A Baltimore citizen leader cites the improved tax base, neighborhood stability, and the improved appearance of the city as three major
benefits of homesteading.

Benefits to Homesteader

All Baltimore homesteaders responding see the program as
beneficial to the city; 100 percent of the homesteaders interviewed
said that they would recommend homesteading to other citizens.

How do the homesteaders feel about their experiences in the
program? In terms of personal satisfaction, 86 percent responded
positively, 60 percent saying they derived "a great deal" of satisfaction and 26 percent derived "some" satisfaction from the program.
Three were pleased with the "adventure"; four received satisfaction
from the "ability to help the inner city"; six were happy with "the
opportunity to own a home"; four were glad "to restore Baltimore's
heritage." Many homesteaders commented on the eased financial
burden and lowered living costs. A heightened social awareness
was expressed by several homesteaders: "I've learned a lot about
the urban social and political scene." "I've learned to relate to
different people." "A closer relation to a community." "A beau-
tiful home; terrific neighbors." These are some of the immeasurable
benefits.

BUFFALO, NEW YORK

Background

In the fall of 1974 Buffalo, New York adopted urban homesteading.
The goals of its program are twofold: to stabilize viable residential
neighborhoods and to provide housing opportunities to low- and
moderate-income families. Two civic-leader questionnaires were
sent and one returned. One questionnaire sent to a homesteading

TABLE 5.1

Comparative Data for Baltimore

	City[a]		Homesteader		
				Survey Data	City-Acquired Data[b]
					Stirling Street	Scattered Sites
Population	906,000	Number of homesteader responses	16	n.a.[c]	n.a.
Percent black	46.4	Percent black	40	49.5	(combined)
Mean income	$10,035	Mean income	$15,400	$17,182	$14,407
Total housing units	305,501	Mean age	31–40	32	(combined)
Substandard units	5,355	Number of homesteads	105	25	85
Units over 30 years old	182,931	Mean rehabilitation costs	—	$26,400	$13,809
Mean housing value (before rehabilitation)	$10,000	Mean housing value (before rehabilitation)	—	$1,311	$3,500
Percent overcrowded[d]	8	Mean family size	2.2	2.6	(combined)

[a] U.S. Bureau of the Census, 1970.
[b] Baltimore Department of Housing and Community Development, Annual Report (Baltimore, Md.: 1974).
[c] n.a. = not applicable.
[d] Overcrowded refers to more than one person per room.
Source: Compiled by the authors.

TABLE 5.2

Baltimore, Maryland Homesteader Path,
REAL Loan and Conventional Loans

Event	Actor	Time
Application filed	Homesteader	—
Interview Held	Awards committee	—
Applicant certified	Housing commissioner	—
Selection of contractor	DHCD/homesteader	—
Financial arrangements: REAL loan, conventional loan	REAL loan consultants/ homesteader	—
Property conveyance (lease-purchase agreement)	City	—
Major rehabilitation	Contractor/homesteader	—
Inspections	DHCD	—
Code approval	Department of Code Enforcements	—
Occupy property	Homesteader	6 months after conveyance
Complete rehabilitation	Homesteader	—
Complete occupancy	Homesteader	24 months after conveyance
Acquire clear title	City	24 months after conveyance

Source: Compiled by the authors.

TABLE 5.3

Baltimore, Maryland Homesteader Path,
312 Loan Property (Stirling Street)

Event	Actor	Time
Application filed	Homesteader	—
Interview	Homesteader/awards committee	—
Applicant certified	Housing commissioner	—
Acquire clear title	City	—
Financial arrangements: 312 loans	HODP	—
REAL loans	REAL loan committee	
Select contractor	Homesteader	—
Major rehabilitation	Contractor/homesteader	—
Inspections	DHCD	—
Code approval	Department of Code Enforcements	6 months from title acquisition
Occupy property	Homesteader	6 months from title acquisition
Complete rehabilitation	Homesteader	24 months from title acquisition
Complete occupancy requirement	Homesteader	24 months from title acquisition

Source: Compiled by the authors.

TABLE 5.4

Baltimore, Maryland City Path, REAL Loan
and Conventional Loans

Event		Time
Selection of properties	DHCD	—
Rehabilitation analysis ("ball park" estimate)	DHCD	—
Advertisement of properties	HODP	—
Certification of home-steaders	Awards committee	—
Transferral of property (interview)	Housing commissioner	—
Work write-up (complete estimate)	DHCD rehabilitation estimator	3 to 4 weeks after transferral
Selection of contractor	REAL loan committee and homesteader	—
Property conveyance (lease-purchase agreement)	City	—
Inspection	DHCD	6 months after transferral
Title transfer	City	24 months after transferral

Source: Compiled by the authors.

55

official was also returned. The program is till evolving with only one
homesteader rehabilitating a house. Three families are building on
vacant land, and other cleared, vacant land has been given to adjacent property owners. Since the homesteader schedule is appropriate
only for homesteaders who are living in their newly acquired home,
none was sent to the buyers in Buffalo.

Unique Characteristics

Buffalo was settled early and began to expand rapidly with the
opening of the Erie Canal in 1825. It is known for its many trees,
which may account for its frame housing stock. The city adopted
an ordinance for urban homesteading. It was thought that some of
the many abandoned structures could be recycled through this program for the city's taxes and for the needed lower-income housing.
When 300 applicants expressed an interest, it was discovered that
many of these structures were unsuitable. At present the city is
devising a program for earlier transferral of title through donation
or sale to the city before vandalism and deterioration set in.

The houses appropriate for homesteading are defined as city-
owned, vacant, residential one- or two-family structures. About
100 such houses exist. They are obtained through "in Rem" action
(foreclosure) after taxes are owed for at least two years. The criteria
used in selecting the specific homes are structural and financial
feasibility of rehabilitation of the house and location within a viable
neighborhood. The first criterion has presented problems because
of the large stock of frame houses in the city as well as the long
foreclosure proceedings which result in vandalism and deterioration.
There are less than ten that are available for homesteading, with
25 as the maximum number in the future.

Laws and Administration

Urban homesteading is within the Department of Community
Development (DCD). Mr. Thomas J. Murphy is the project manager.
There are four persons in the department who work with the program
on a part-time basis. In the selection of homesteaders, priority is
given to urban-renewal relocatees and area residents. Consideration
is given to the applicants' construction skills and ability to finance
repairs and maintain the property in the future.

Financial Options

The program is implemented with a Community Development block grant. Financial assistance for homesteaders is obtained through commercial home-improvement loans or the City of Buffalo Rehabilitation Loan Fund. The interest rates are generally 8 percent for a five-year loan. The city guarantees the loans for the home-steaders.

Support Services

The urban-homesteading program provides technical assistance to the buyers. Advice on procedures and on selection and supervision of contractors is offered, also. These services are utilized a great deal, but they are not unique to the homesteading program. They are part of the existing city services.

Benefits

The program is so limited and so new that the effects are not yet measurable. The civic-leader response indicated an interest in expanding the program. This is part of the plan, of course, but it necessitates some legal changes, possibly by the state, to acquire the houses in a rehabilitable stage. Mr. Murphy, in a telephone conversation on July 16, 1975, alluded to the complex legal mechanisms under which they operate within the state of New York that make it difficult to implement the program successfully.

CAMDEN, NEW JERSEY

Background

In 1974 a homesteading committee was established in Camden to study the program and its structure in Wilmington and in Philadelphia. An ordinance was passed late in 1974. The goal of the program in Camden was to rehabilitate abandoned residential structures. It would also serve to increase the tax retables for the city, remove deteriorating blight from stable neighborhoods, and add sound housing to the stock of available residential units in the city. [8]

TABLE 5.5

Comparative Data for Buffalo

City*		Homesteaders	
Population	400,000	Number of homesteader responses	0
Mean income	$9,311		
		Number of homesteads	4
Units over 30 years old	86%	Mean rehabilitation costs	$6,000
Mean housing value	$12,800	Mean housing value (before rehabilitation)	$12,000
Average number of persons per room	2.8		

*U.S. Bureau of the Census, 1970.
Source: Compiled by the authors.

TABLE 5.6

Buffalo, New York Homesteader Path

Event	Actor	Time
Application	Homesteader	—
Interview	Homesteader/DCD	—
Property conveyance	DCD	—
Taxes	Homesteader	Immediately, as owner
Financial arrangements	Conventional or city rehabilitation loan fund	—
Rehabilitation	Homesteader/contractor	—
Occupancy	Homesteader	—

Source: Compiled by the authors.

TABLE 5.7

Buffalo, New York City Path

Event	Actor	Time
Certification of homesteaders	DCD	—
Selection of properties	DCD	—
Rehabilitation analysis of properties	DCD	—
Advertisement of properties	DCD	—
Transferral of property to homesteader (interview)	DCD	—
Property conveyance	DCD	At interview
Support services	DCD	Throughout homesteading period

Source: Compiled by the authors.

The high number of abandoned buildings within the city was a motivating factor in creating an interest in an urban-homesteading program. The city has largely older housing units. The vacancies, rather high, can be assumed to include many of these structures.[9] Median value of homes is relatively low.[10] Hence, the demand for housing for the middle-income range must not be great, but very tight for low and moderate income. The houses could probably be rehabilitated at a relatively low cost. Information furnished by the city shows the work write-ups for two houses.[11] One requires $1,500 and the other $500 of contracted work and materials to meet the code standards.

The abandoned properties included in the program are owned by the city. They are sold at auction to qualified homesteaders. The minimum bid is $100.

There are five homesteaders as of July 1975, according to Mrs. Barbara Broadwater, administrative assistant to the mayor. Twelve are in the process of acquiring houses. Five homesteader question-naires were sent to Mrs. Broadwater for distribution. Three official and two civic-leader questionnaires were also mailed to Camden. Only two homesteaders responded.

Unique Characteristics

The city was incorporated in 1828 but began to be settled as early as 1680. It has been an important industrial center for 200 years. As it has expanded, the older, inner-city area has deteriorated.

Laws and Administration

New Jersey law as described in the Newark section applies likewise to Camden. The ordinance passed by the city council established a real-estate board of nine members.[12] It is govern-ment centered with all but the chairman as specific city employees. Members of the board include representatives of the Office of Planning and Renewal: Department of Community Relations; Depart-ment of Building Inspector, Division of Housing; City Properties; Law Department; Office of Intergovernmental Relations; and mayor's office. The chairman of the Homesteading Subcommittee is a member of its parent committee, the Mayor's Citizen Advisory Committee. The board's duties are to maintain a list of unoccupied city-owned structures suitable for rehabilitation, to prepare a list for the city council of criteria for evaluating an individual's rehabilitation abilities, to consult with and to evaluate all applicants for homesteading, and to advise the council whether the highest bidder meets the criteria. The buyer must be at least 18 years old and must demonstrate, within two weeks of sale, the ability to rehabilitate or to finance rehabilitation. The city council approves the purchases, and the sale is finalized.

The potential buyer agrees to the work write-up items. After the sale is completed, a conditional title is given to the buyer. It may be rescinded by the city if the buyer does not meet the program requirements. The selected homesteader contracts the work or does the work himself. Rehabilitation must be completed in six months (with a possible six-month extension.)

A certificate for occupancy should be issued within six months of the sale. The homesteader begins to live in the house within one month of occupancy certification. The required homestead period is three years from date of occupancy. If the homesteader desires a clear deed title, he must order a title search and pay for it.

Any adult 18 or older, who will rehabilitate and maintain the house at city-code standards, live in it for three years, and give proof of resources before final purchase and settlement, may become an eligible homesteader. This final criterion is most important.

The two respondents to the homesteader schedule survey are black female single parents with children. Both estimate their take-home pay at $6,000. They are using personal savings. Both are over 30 years old and presumably have been saving money for several years.

Financial Options and Support Services

There are no loan arrangements. Technical assistance is offered by the board and the staff. The staff has eight persons: homestead coordinator, assistant coordinator, administrative assistant, rehabilitation specialist, bilingual coordinator, housing development specialists (two), and a secretary.

Benefits

The two homesteader respondents were pleased with the program and its low-cost homeownership. Locating contractors and financing have been problems. One noted a benefit of being able to help the city and herself. Both commented favorably on the help and availability of the homestead staff. They felt the program was well run.

TABLE 5.8

Comparative Data for Camden

City*		Homesteader	
Population	102,551	Number of homesteader responses	2
		Number black	2
		Mean income	$6,000
		Mean age	31–40
Units over 30 years old	70%	Number of homesteads	5
Mean housing value	$8,400	Mean rehabilitation costs	$1,000
Average number of persons per room	3.1		

*U.S. Bureau of the Census, 1970.
<u>Source</u>: Compiled by the authors.

TABLE 5.9

Camden, New Jersey Homesteader Path

Event	Actor	Time
Application	Homesteader	After advertisement
Interview	Homesteader real-estate board	—
Property conveyance (auction— conditional title)	City council	—
Financial arrangement	Conventional loan or personal savings	—
Rehabilitation	Contractor/homesteader	6 months (possible 6-month extension)
Inspections and approval for occupancy	City	6 months
Settlement of deed	City	After rehabilitation
Taxes	Homesteader	After settlement
Occupy property	Homesteader	Within 1 month of approval
Complete occupancy requirement	Homesteader	3 years from date of occupancy
Acquire clear title	Homesteader pays for title search	Anytime

<u>Source</u>: Compiled by the authors.

TABLE 5.10

Camden, New Jersey City Path

Event	Actor	Time
Selection of properties	Real-estate board	—
Rehabilitation analysis of properties	City	—
Advertisement of properties	City	—
Transferral of properties to homesteaders (auction)	City	—
Certification of homesteaders	Real-estate board/city council	Within 2 weeks after sale
Property conveyance (conditional title)	City council	After certification
Inspection for complete rehabilitation	City	6 months (possible 6-month extension)
Certificate for occupancy	City	Within 6 months of sale
Settlement of deed	City	After rehabilitation
Periodic inspections	City	During occupancy

<u>Source</u>: Compiled by the authors.

61

MINNEAPOLIS, MINNESOTA

Background

A bill enacted by the Minnesota state legislature during the 1974 session made urban homesteading possible in Minneapolis. [13] The city was given the authority to sell city-owned abandoned houses or open land to low- and moderate-income persons for less than the fair-market value. The buyers were given a specified time period in which to bring the house up to code or to complete new construction. The property was then deeded to the homesteader.

Administrative guidelines were adopted in November 1974. [14] The goals of the program in Minneapolis are as follows:

1. Revitalize neighborhoods by increasing their economic vitality.
2. Stimulate housing rehabilitation where it would not otherwise occur.
3. Offer a homeownership opportunity for those who could not otherwise afford it.
4. Increase the tax productivity of residential properties.
5. Reduce hazards created by vacant structures. [15]

Urban homesteading is one part of the overall plan to revitalize neighborhoods.

The income requirements for the program were publicized. Therefore, it would seem that applicants for the homesteading program might reflect the profile of the eventual homesteaders fairly accurately in income level. The Minneapolis Housing and Redevelopment Authority (MHRA) formed such a profile of applicants for each sale. [16] The following facts are taken from these reports. In the first lottery for one house, there were 106 applicants with the median income at $9,000. The next three homes had 243 applicants of which 217 were eligible. The median income of the eligible applicants was $7,000 to $9,000. The principal group to benefit from the program is the $10,000-to-$15,000 group, according to an official within the program. The two homesteaders to respond to our questionnaire have incomes of $12,000 and $12,500. It would seem that the program is geared toward the moderate-income group. The loans required ranged from $11,300 to $14,750. Sweat equity covered the rest of the costs. Sweat equity is the equity earned by a homeowner from improvements he has made personally. This applies to homesteaders attempting to rehabilitate a house almost entirely themselves. The value of sweat equity is determined by the sale price of the house when completed. Responses to the officials' questionnaire give the resale values, after rehabilitation, as varying from $15,000 to $26,800 with the median at $17,900. This corresponds exactly with the median value of owner-occupied homes in 1970. Since the national real-estate market value has increased at 5 percent each year, the homesteaded value will be a moderately priced house. Such totally dilapidated housing could only be rehabilitated by moderate-income persons who have the financial means of meeting such loan payments. Higher-quality housing, however, would carry a higher sale price. In order to make the program more accessible to lower-income persons, MHRA has stated in its literature that it is trying to obtain funds to offset these costs and offer the houses for less.

Unique Characteristics

The action of the state legislature enabled Minneapolis to adopt this program. Its feasibility is enhanced with availability of locally financed loans at low interest rates. In some cases, the cost of the property is the cost of acquisition. This may be included in the loan. Such attractive financial arrangements encourage homesteading in this city.

Laws and Administration

The Minnesota legislature authorized the city of Minneapolis to sell $10,000,000 of general-obligation bonds to finance a housing-rehabilitation loan-and-grant program.[17] This was based on the recognition of a need for housing-rehabilitation programs in Minneapolis and the fact that conventional loans are too expensive and too difficult to obtain for many homeowners. The provisions stipulate that the city consider the needs of the house, the income of the applicant, the type of house (regular single-family or homestead), and other loans available.

The availability of loans plus the authority to sell below market value made homesteading in Minneapolis feasible.

The Housing and Redevelopment Authority administers the program for the city. A steering committee was established by the authority with representatives of community groups, private citizens, and public officials as members. Its role is to establish administrative guidelines and monitor their implementation. Our correspondence has been with Donald A. D. Snyder, planner.

The urban homesteading is a two-stage program. The first stage is a demonstration project with a limited number of houses in scattered sites. An evaluation of the procedures will be made to determine

the effectiveness of the program. This may lead to an expansion of
the city's commitment to urban homesteading.

In response to the questionnaire administered to officials, the
administrative costs and related expenses for the program were
stated as budgeted at $2,500 for each property. With nine properties
now in the program, the total cost is around $22,500 to the authority.
This does not reflect the expenses and tax losses no longer incurred
by other city agencies in maintaining the properties in an abandoned
state, however. The properties are leased to homesteaders with the
title held by MHRA, until rehabilitation is complete. The homesteader
then receives a fee-simple title.

The homesteader applicants must meet certain criteria: "Be a
resident of Minneapolis for at least 90 days before applying; be at
least 18 years of age; be a person or family of low or moderate
income."[18] A scale has been established of family size with maximum annual gross income for eligibility. In addition, the applicant's
ability to repay loan and ability to rehabilitate the house are considered by the steering committee and the authority. Efforts are made
to offer homesteading opportunities to persons in public housing or
persons displaced by public projects. Nonprofit housing corporations
are eligible if there is a guarantee that the housing will be for low-
or moderate-income persons.

The names of applicants meeting these requirements are put in a
lottery receptacle. At the first lottery, 21 names are drawn. These
include seven residing in public housing, seven residing in the
general neighborhood where the homestead property is located, and
seven from other parts of the city.

The authority, with interested neighborhood-organization representatives, considers the 21 applicants (without violating their
privacy rights). If more than one could qualify, a second lottery is
held to determine who the homesteader will be.

An investigation of available land is carried out by the authority
for possible properties to be used in the program. Within each land
category, vacant houses are given priority as homestead sites. The
eventual use of the house must be in compliance with all the city
regulations for that area. Fair-market value of the house after
rehabilitation must be higher than acquisition and rehabilitation
costs. The cost estimates and needed work are advertised when the
house is offered for homesteading.

The homestead period is three years from the granting of the
fee-simple title. If a homesteader should sell before this period is
completed, the authority would receive a portion of the money. The
price of the house is established according to the acquisition costs,
until additional funds become available to absorb a difference in
cost and sale price.

Financial Options

Federal and locally financed loans are available to eligible homesteaders. These have interest rates of 4 percent, 6 percent, or
8 percent, according to combined income of household.

Taxes and insurance are paid on the house each month by the
homesteader, once he or she has completed the rehabilitation and
received a fee-simple title. If a homesteader should have to vacate
early, the authority aids the owner in recovering the investment.

Support Services

After the lottery selection of the homesteader the authority
provides counseling to explain the program requirements. The
"homesteader's agreement" is discussed and target dates established
for the public hearing required for sale of the property, the MHRA
Board of Commissioners action, the property conveyance, the loan
arrangements, work commencement, and occupancy. After the
public hearing, the homesteader's agreement is executed.

Neighborhood organizations and MHRA assist in locating technical
expertise to aid the homesteader using sweat equity. The MHRA has
an arrangement with the Inspections Department to assist homesteaders in making sound repairs. The rehabilitation counselor from
MHRA makes periodic inspections, also. The loan payments are not
required until the second month after the date the house is certified
for occupancy.

Another support service with a broader effect is in the form of
a policy guideline. The authority has a provision that guarantees
minority contractors and subcontractors equal opportunity to perform the rehabilitation work. All contractors are required to be
equal-opportunity employers.

Benefits

Although the program is too new to assess in terms of specific
benefits, a civic leader responded in a questionnaire that homesteading does benefit Minneapolis financially, socially, and cosmetically. One of the goals is to offer homeownership opportunities
to those unable to afford it otherwise. The response of one home
steader indicates that this goal is being realized in his or her case.
The staff was described as very helpful, but the paperwork required
tends to make the program ponderous.

TABLE 5.11

Comparative Data for Minneapolis

	City[a]	Homesteader
Population	434,000	2
Number of homesteader responses		
Median income	$10,567[b]	
Mean income[c]		$12,250 $8,000
Units over 30 years old	68%	
Average rehabilitation costs		$13,025
Median value of housing	$17,900	
Mean housing value (after rehabilitation)		$17,900
Average number of persons per room	2.6	

[a]U.S. Bureau of the Census, 1970.
[b]This figure is for the entire Minneapolis/St. Paul Standard Metropolitan Statistical Area.
[c] The first figure is the average income of homesteaders surveyed. The second figure is the median income of the eligible applicants for homesteading.

<u>Source:</u> Compiled by the authors.

TABLE 5.12

Minneapolis, Minnesota Homesteader Path

Event	Actor	Time
Application	Homesteader	After advertisement
Interview	Homesteader/MHRA	After first and second lottery
Property conveyance and homesteader agreement	Homesteader/MHRA	—
Financial arrangements	Conventional, city, or federal government loan	—
Major rehabilitation commences	Homesteader/contractor	Within 30 days of agreement
Completed	Homesteader/contractor	90 days later
Approval for occupancy	MRHA	After major rehabilitation
Occupancy	Homesteader	After approval
Complete rehabilitation	Contractor	180 days after agreement
	Homesteader	2 years after agreement
	(HUD house) homesteader	1 1/2 years after commencement
Receive fee-simple title	Homesteader	After rehabilitation
Taxes	Homesteader	After title
Occupancy period	Homesteader	3 years from title

Source: Compiled by the authors.

TABLE 5.13

Minneapolis, Minnesota City Path

Event	Actor	Time
Selection of properties	MHRA	—
Rehabilitation analysis of properties	MHRA	—
Advertisement of properties	MHRA	—
Certification of homesteaders	MHRA/steering committee (neighborhood organization)	—
Transferral of property to homesteaders(lottery)	MHRA Board of Commissioners public hearing	—
Property conveyance and homesteader agreement	MHRA	After board action
Support services	MHRA counselors	Throughout total process
Inspections	Inspections Department MHRA counselors	Periodic
Certificate of completion fee-simple title	MHRA	After rehabilitation

Source: Compiled by the authors.

NEWARK, NEW JERSEY

Background

The Newark homesteading program was begun in 1974. Much research went into the planning stage. Steven C. Rother, Newark tax collector at that time, addressed several of the inherent problems and their relationship to New Jersey law in an article published in New Jersey Municipalities in January 1974.[19] The thrust of the concept, to him, came from abandonment rather than housing needs or neighborhood preservation. Existing New Jersey statutes also make this approach the more facile one.

Several attempts to obtain information on the Newark plan were unsuccessful, partially because of personnel changes in city hall; the official and homesteader questionnaires were misdirected by temporary employees. Only the civic leaders returned the schedules. Ten homesteader questionnaires were sent initially. A telephone follow-up to the temporary tax collector revealed the confusion. He said there are about 300 homesteaders in Newark. Yet, Newark has thousands of abandoned buildings. The population declined 22,803 in the previous decade.[20] The abandonment rate is probably this high because much of the population is moving to the suburbs of this, the largest city in New Jersey.

Unique Characteristics

New Jersey law allows owners to deed properties to the city in lieu of foreclosure, a source of about 100 houses a year in Newark. In 1972, "in Rem" (foreclosure) procedures gave the city title to 1,200 properties; in 1973, the city acquired an additional 500.[21] These do not include VA and FHA mortgage foreclosures, possibly higher-quality houses. They met rigid United States standards before being sold to the present owners; when there is a mortgage failure, they are vacated to meet insurance regulations. If the federal regulation on sales of these houses at market value were waived, these could become part of the homesteading stock for little consideration.

The New Jersey statute regulating sales by municipalities allows broad freedom in establishing conditions. Specific homesteading requirements can be applied to all buyers of the selected homestead properties. There is a requirement, however, that cities sell to the highest bidder (eliminating the possibility of one dollar houses).

Financing by the city is legal. The interest must be the higher current rate (8 percent in 1974) of either the usury statute or municipal bonds. Rother suggests that since the mortgage may not exceed five years, a "balloon" payment at the end be refinanced conventionally. A balloon payment is the final payment of a large, short-term loan. It amounts to the bulk of the loan itself. This practice allows low monthly payments until the final one, which then could be refinanced as a long-term loan. It is useful for borrowers who need to build credit for low-interest, long-term loans. The rehabilitated home can be used as an asset.

Laws and Administration

The Newark urban-homesteading program is a part of the Department of Tax Collection. There are two approaches used by the city. Some houses have major rehabilitation done by city-supervised contractors. These are then auctioned for the minimum price of renovation costs. Unrepaired houses are auctioned for $100 to $500. Much advertisement and "hoopla" accompanies the auctions. There is a one-year limit for rehabilitation and a five-year requirement for occupancy.[22] Around 300 houses are in various stages of rehabilitation by homesteaders.

The financing of rehabilitation would be limiting because of statute requirements. One civic leader suggested a change in the program to provide better financing for the buyer, with either federal or state support.

Benefits

Both civic leaders claim homesteading is beneficial for the city of Newark. They see the program as helping the city financially, improving neighborhood stability and citizen attitudes, and improving city appearance. Neither knows of any change in real-estate values or private preservation efforts attributable to homesteading, but both believe that it has the potential of preventing further neighborhood abandonment and deterioration.

These responses indicate that the goals have been in line with Rother's. As he stated in his article, "The goal of homesteading shouldn't be to sell dilapidated buildings for one dollar each, but rather to assure the occupancy and upgrading of abandoned buildings."[23]

TABLE 5.14

Census Data for Newark

Population	382,417
Median income	$10,658
Units over 30 years old	68%
Median value of housing	$17,300
Average persons per room	3.1

Source: Compiled by the authors.

TABLE 5.15

Newark, New Jersey Homesteader Path

Event	Actor	Time
Property conveyance (auction)	Tax dept.	—
Financial arrangement	Conventional loan or personal savings	—
Rehabilitation	Homesteader/contractor	1 year
Complete occupancy requirement	Homesteader	5 years

Source: Compiled by the authors.

TABLE 5.16

Newark, New Jersey City Path

Event	Actor	Time
Selection of properties	Tax dept.	—
Rehabilitation analysis	Tax dept.	—
Major rehabilitation of some properties	City-supervised contractors	—
Advertisement of properties	Tax dept.	—
Transferral of property to homesteader (auction)	Tax dept.	—
Property conveyance	Tax dept.	At auction

Source: Compiled by the authors.

PHILADELPHIA, PENNSYLVANIA

Background

Joseph Coleman, Philadelphia councilman and chairman of the Urban Homestead Board, began to formulate the concept of urban homesteading in the mid-60s. (Many writers and students credit him with originating the concept. See Chapter 3.) In 1968 he proposed urban homesteading in a paper presented to the Philadelphia Planning Commission.

The City of Philadelphia enacted urban homesteading in an ordinance that was passed on July 26, 1973. It was not until July 1, 1974 that the program was funded and began implementation. During that year the Urban Homestead Board worked with a temporary staff, loaned from other city housing agencies, to develop the program.

A nonprofit finance corporation was created to supply short-term construction funds. The corporation was supported by church groups, social-welfare organizations, and representatives from the financial community. This private-sector organization gave impetus to the program. Many participants and observers consider that the involvement of the private sector is pivotal to the Philadelphia program.[24] "The history of urban homesteading is one of breakthrough coordination between the public and private sectors and among government agencies to address the problems of urban neighborhood viability and housing abandonment."[25]

"The goal of Philadelphia's urban homesteading program is to provide persons in need of housing with ownership of a home."[26] The program focuses on individuals in need of housing as well as on neighborhoods or blocks. Homesteading officials in Philadelphia stress the fact that homesteading is but one approach to neighborhood stabilization. It is not the only, nor is it the final, solution to the city's housing crisis. They also stress that it should be integrated into an overall city housing policy. "Urban homesteading will play a helpful role in limited areas. It is not a panacea."[27] According to Time magazine, there are 36,000 abandoned homes in Philadelphia.[28] At least 50 percent of these are in good enough condition to be rehabilitated.

Guidelines for evaluating the suitability of areas for homesteading were developed by the board during the intervening year. It is estimated that the number of vacant and deteriorated structures in Philadelphia ranges from 20,000 to 35,000.[29] This large number of houses, spread throughout the city, made it necessary for the board to select specific areas and sites for initiating the program.

Philadelphia had done considerable work in the area of neighborhood typologies. This work proved useful in deciding where urban homesteading could be implemented. The guidelines devised were based on a classification scheme that termed neighborhood abandonment as mild, moderate, or severe.

Ultimately, the designation of homestead areas derived from the following formula: vacancy rates of less than 5 percent, more than 65 percent homeownership, and property values ranging from $8,000 to $12,000. Other neighborhoods could be included if they had strong block or neighborhood organizations or if they gave evidence that publi or private rehabilitation efforts were under way.

The specific property selection is based on the amount of rehabilitation work that is required. Houses with serious structural defects are not considered suitable. One criteria of suitability is the estimate cost of rehabilitation. Houses must be rehabilitable at or below their fair-market value. There are some exceptions. Other criteria are current ownership and community interest in the program.

Currently, the city of Philadelphia, the Redevelopment Authority, and the Philadelphia Housing Authority own hundreds of abandoned houses. Many of these are considered too deteriorated to be used for homesteading. Acquisition of other abandoned properties is accomplished by eminent domain (condemned by the Redevelopment Authority by sheriff's sale (city bids in tax-delinquent properties), or by a meth Philadelphia has devised. Through it people can give their tax-delinquent homes to the city, be relieved of their tax responsibility, and take a tax write-off for the gift. In this way Philadelphia has received several hundred homes. The other two methods are rarely used.

The Urban Homestead Board was not empowered to own or acquire properties. The Philadelphia city charter required that the city council sell properties to the "best bidder." Since homestead properties are sold for one dollar, it was necessary to create a structure through which properties could be transferred to a homesteader. The transferring authority is the Philadelphia Housing Development Corporation (PHDC). The homestead board has developed a mechanism for property acquisition. City-owned property, held by the Public Property Department, is transferred to the Redevelopment Authority and by them to the PHDC. Gifts of property are made directly to the PHDC. FHA property is sold to the PHDC.

In all three cases the PHDC acquires and owns the property and then transfers it to the homesteader. For fiscal 1975, the city council has authorized $1.5 million in capital funds to the Urban Homestead Board for the purchase of homes, lead-paint removal, and loan guarantees. Approximately $100,000 is available for the purchase of FHA properties at prices ranging from $1 to $5,000. The board believes that this will assure a high quality inventory.

In August of 1974, 20 properties were awarded to the first urban homesteaders in Philadelphia. By the end of the first year, 74 parcels had been brought into the Urban Homestead Program. Thirty-one of these have been completely rehabilitated and are occupied. Fourteen other homesteaders have been designated, and rehabilitation of the properties is in progress. The remaining properties have been advertised. Over 2,000 applications have been filed for homesteads.

Thirty-one homesteader schedules were sent to the staff associate director, Jan Jaffe, along with a homestead-official schedule. Only the official schedule was completed and returned. The homesteader forms were not distributed. One civic-leader schedule was returned from the chamber of commerce.

Unique Characteristics

The City Council of Philadelphia has provided almost $2 million in capital funds for an urban-homestead program. The scope and implications of this commitment are unique among homestead cities. This funding, in addition to considerable private-sector support, as well as already on-going neighborhood stabilization programs, comprises a package of unique factors within Philadelphia's homestead program. The initial thrust of private-sector participation was to provide the funds for short-term rehabilitation loans. These funds are funneled through the Urban Homestead Finance Corporation. The funds were donated mainly by the Episcopal Diocese and the Penn National Bank. Private-sector participation in other aspects of the program is also planned.

Other unique characteristics should be noted. The number of abandoned homes in Philadelphia is a problem of immense proportions. Urban homesteading, which deals mainly in abandoned houses, can plan an extensive life-span in a city with a potential stock of this size. The character of the architecture is another special feature in Philadelphia. An abundance of brick row houses makes the cost of rehabilitation and maintenance possible for low- and moderate-income applicants. The influence of Councilman Joseph Coleman lends special qualities to the Philadelphia program. His philosophy has influenced the direction the program has taken. The program is approached comprehensively, working with homesteaders as well as with the surrounding environment. Participation comes from all sectors of the city: city government, Bell Telephone, State Department of Community Affairs, Penn Housing Finance Agency, citizen groups, and housing coalitions. It is a determined, united effort to revitalize neighborhoods.

Laws and Administration

Four major documents relate to urban homesteading in Philadelphia: Bill C543, the first homestead ordinance, which was approved on July 20, 1973; Resolution 333, which provided $1.5 million for urban homesteading for the year 1975; Bill 961 of January 28, 1974, which allowed tax exemption from real property tax on assessed valuation of improvements to buildings and structures (This is a graduated exemption which terminates after five years. The first year's exemption is 100 percent. Every succeeding year the exemption is 20 percent less.); and Bill 1664, an amended homestead ordinance which was passed February 6, 1975.[30] This last ordinance created a homestead board of 11 members. It stipulated that the board be appointed by the mayor, recommended by the city council, and serve a term of three years without compensation. It also provided that the board include at least one architect, one contractor or member of the building-trades council, one clergyman, one representative from a financial institution, two representatives from the general public, and two members of the city council. This revised ordinance corrected many of the flaws that were pointed out in an issue of the Buffalo Law Review.[31]

The revised ordinance outlined 20 extensive duties for the board. It gave the Philadelphia board broad powers not held by boards in most other cities. Although the board may not hold title to property, it has the power to recommend foreclosures by instituting nuisance procedures. The duties also included the monitoring of abandoned properties and extensive services to homesteaders.

The administration is funded for $219,000 each year. The homestead board hires the administrative staff which at present consists of 11 people: the executive director, 2 assistant directors, a rehabilitation coordinator, a community-resources coordinator, a housing-rehabilitation technician, a bilingual housing-rehabilitation technician, a bilingual area housing worker, a program-services officer, a clerk stenographer, and a clerk typist.

Homesteaders are selected on the basis of the following criteria:

1. Twenty-one-years old or head of a household.
2. Non-profit community organizations.
3. Citizen of the United States or with declared intentions to become one.
4. Proven financial ability and/or access to building-trade skills.
5. Willing to build or rehabilitate to code standards beginning within 60 days after title has been acquired.
6. Willing to live on and occupy structure for not less than 5 years.

7. A nonprofit organization must be willing to provide services to that community for not less than 5 years.

8. Willing to fulfill other requirements deemed necessary by homestead board.

An administrative decision of the board gives special consideration to applicants who demonstrate a need for better housing. This includes those living in substandard housing, those living in overcrowded housing, those subject to eviction because of government action or urban renewal, and those paying too much for their current unit (more than 25 percent of their annual income). Whenever possible, those who live near prospective sites are given first priority.

The staff ranks all applicants on the basis of interviews and presents its recommendations to the homestead board. The final screening takes place at an open house at the specific property.

Financial Options

The Philadelphia Urban Homestead Board recognizes the need for a flexible financial package for each homesteader. Initially the homestead board uses limited capital funds to replace some systems, such as wiring, and to reduce the cost to the homesteader where the rehabilitation costs exceed the market value of the house. Short-term construction funds are supplied through the Urban Homestead Financial Corporation. These notes are sold at 6 percent for a five year term. When the work is completed satisfactorily, the Pennsylvania Housing Finance Agency (PHFA) has agreed to take out these short-term loans and to provide low-interest (1 to 8 percent depending on income level), long-term (15 year) loans. Long-term mortages are also available from several local banks. The PHFA has created a $250,000 fund for this purpose dependent on the success of the program plus a commitment from private sources in Philadelphia. A tax-abatement program is also provided according to Bill 961, as referred to above.

Support Services

The support services offered by Philadelphia include loan subsidies, improved city services, housing management counseling, private-sector financial commitment, community participation in selection and planning, a neighborhood parks program, a mechanism to guarantee integrity of all contractors, and community homestead-advisory

TABLE 5.17

Comparative Data for Philadelphia

City[a]		Homesteader[c]	
Population	1,948,609	Number of homesteaders	74
Average family income	$10,431	Average income	$9,170
Percent black	33.6%	Average family size	4
Total housing units	673,524	Average age	34
Substandard units	15,615	Came from substandard units	50%
Percent overcrowded[b]	6.3%	Came from overcrowded	75%
Units over 30 years old	69%	Average cost of rehabilitation	$7,000

[a]U.S. Bureau of the Census, 1970.
[b]Overcrowded refers to more than one person per room.
[c]The Philadelphia Partnership, "Urban Homesteading," p. 6.
Source: Compiled by the authors.

TABLE 5.18

Philadelphia, Pennsylvania Homesteader Path

Event	Actor	Time
Application filed	Homesteader	—
Interview held	Homestead staff/homesteader	—
Property conveyance (clear title)	Homestead board	—
Major rehabilitation plan, financial arrangements, select contractor (board certified)	Homestead staff/homesteader	2 months after conveyance
Inspections	Homestead staff	—
Approval for occupancy	Dept. of Licences and Inspections	4 months after conveyance
Occupy property	Homesteader	4 months after conveyance
Complete rehabilitation	Homesteader	24 months after conveyance
Code approval	Dept. of Licenses and Inspections	24 months after conveyance
Complete occupancy requirements	Homesteader	5 years after occupying

Source: Compiled by the authors.

TABLE 5.19

Philadelphia, Pennsylvania City Path

Event	Actor	Time
Selection of properties	Homestead staff	—
Advertisement of properties	Homestead staff	—
Certification of homesteader	Homestead staff	—
Rehabilitation analysis	Homestead staff	—
Transferral of property (open house)	Homestead board	—
Property conveyance (clear title)	Homestead board	—
Work write-up/loan and contractor	Homestead staff	60 days after conveyance
Inspection of work	Dept. of Licenses and Inspections	60 days after conveyance
Final inspection	Dept. of Licenses and Inspections	2 years after conveyance

Source: Compiled by the authors.

councils formed in each homestead neighborhood. These affect
every area of homesteading. At least one year of study preceded
the initiation of these services. They were a cornerstone of its program since it is directed to the ill-housed.

Benefits

Neighborhood stability was the benefit most significant to one
citizen leader who responded to the questionnaire. One of the homesteading officials commented on the benefits to Philadelphia: "Homesteading offers an opportunity to rekindle the pride and spirit of
many families and communities. It will be an important element in
rebuilding the residential areas of the city. . . . The program should
not be construed as a revolutionary approach or a solution to our
housing problems."

PITTSBURGH, PENNSYLVANIA

Background

The City Urban Homestead Program was initiated in November
1973. It was established as the result of an executive decision of the
mayor, Pete Flaherty. There is no homestead ordinance in Pittsburgh—no specific board or staff responsible for the program. The
homestead program is administered by the city Real Estate Division
of the Department of Lands and Buildings and the city Urban Redevelopment Authority. In response to the questionnaire, one program official
said that the goal of the program is "to reduce the amount of property
owned by the city and return property to the tax rolls."

There are two groups of houses presently in Pittsburgh's homestead program. One group is comprised of 400 tax-delinquent and
unoccupied units. These units will be sold under the homesteading
program for the cost of transfer. Additionally, the city is trustee for
250 tax-delinquent properties that are owned jointly by the city, the
school board, and Allegheny County. These properties are occupied;
the families who reside in them pay the city a monthly amount that
covers the taxes that would be due on the properties. The homestead
program is attempting to sell these properties to their present occupants. Ten units have been conveyed in this way.

Forty-eight questionnaires for homesteaders were sent to Pittsburgh for distribution. Only two of these forms were returned. There
seems to be some confusion among these households about their
designation as homesteaders. This is probably due to the fact that

many of them are rehabilitating houses that they formerly occupied
as renters. Their designation as homesteaders was an administrative decision that came after the fact. One official questionnaire was
completed and returned.

Unique Characteristics

According to the Pittsburgh housing official who returned the
questionnaire schedule, Pittsburgh has an abundance of low-cost
housing available. The respondent considered that fact as a deterrent to the success of homesteading. Since many other cities have
similarly priced homes available, the demand in Pittsburgh may
be less. This demand factor appears to be the consideration this
official is stressing. However, he also stated that the occupied
houses in the program are of brick construction. The tax-delinquent
properties in the homestead program that are occupied should
therefore be less costly to rehabilitate and maintain because of
their construction and because occupied housing usually suffers
less deterioration than vacant housing.

The fact that Pittsburgh's homestead program enables a renter
to own the home he occupies is very unique to homesteading. Neighborhood residents are given first priority for the vacant homes.
This aspect of the Pittsburgh program is also unique.

Laws and Administration

Although there is no official homestead ordinance in Pittsburgh,
there is a tax-abatement law that was designed specifically to
encourage families to participate in the City Urban Homestead
Program. The law provides that taxes be abated for a three year
period for improvements up to $10,000.

The state of Pennsylvania has passed enabling legislation that
raises the debt level for Pittsburgh. This legislation has empowered
the city to vote a bond referendum to be used for low-interest
rehabilitation loans.

The city is attempting to persuade the state legislature to provide
direct funding for a low-interest loan program. This effort is based
on the theory that municipal budgets are already strained and that
the broader tax base of the Commonwealth of Pennsylvania must be
utilized to provide funds for the homestead program. [32]

Currently the homestead program has no specific administra-
tive structure or budget. It is operated through the Real Estate
Division, Department of Lands and Buildings and through the Urban
Redevelopment Authority.

As stated above, first priority for homesteaders is given to
neighborhood residents. City residents are given second priority,
and all others are qualified last. These priorities are based on
the proviso that the homesteader has the financial ability to rehabilitate the property. Financial ability takes precedence over all other
priorities.

Financial Options

Pittsburgh has provided low-interest loans in three neighborhoods. These loans are essential where the city is attempting to
get present renters to buy and rehabilitate their properties. The
program in Central North Side is financed with $500,000 in Scaife
Foundation funds (a private foundation). In the Model Cities areas
there is a $300,000 Model Cities Fund. The program in Garfield
is funded by a $2 million Federal Code Enforcement Fund. Home-
steaders in other areas must procure conventional financing.
The city is now working on a citywide low-interest-loan program.
Testimony in the state legislature indicated that Pittsburgh is filing
application for $800,000 in matching funds for this loan program.[33]
The terms of the above loans range up to 20 years. Pittsburgh has
arranged for total tax abatement for a three-year period.

Support Services

Pittsburgh provides several services through various city
departments to homestead applicants. The Real Estate Division
mails property listings and provides specific information about houses
available in the program. The Urban Redevelopment Authority
provides a work write-up, indicating code violations that must be
abated and the estimated cost of the work. The Urban Redevelopment Authority works with the applicant to verify financial
ability and/or skills to perform necessary work. In some neighborhoods, the Neighborhood Housing Service helps applicants to procure
low-interest-loan and grant money.

Benefits

Responding to a question about the success of homesteading in
Pittsburgh, one official says he considers the program "somewhat
successful."

TABLE 5.20

Comparative Data for Pittsburgh

City*		Homesteader	
Population	520,146	Number of home- steader responses	2
Mean income	$10,536		
Total housing units	189,840	Number of home- steaders	48
Substandard units	13,442	Cost of rehabilita- tion	$8,000– $9,000
Percent overcrowded	6%	Estimated housing value (after rehabili- tation	$11,000– $12,000
Median value of housing	$12,500		
Percent units over 30 year old	79%		

*U.S. Bureau of Census, 1970.
Source: Compiled by the authors.

TABLE 5.21

Pittsburgh, Pennsylvania Homesteader Path

Event	Actor	Time
Application filed	Homesteader/Real Estate Division	—
Major rehabilitation plan	Urban Redevelopment Authority	—
Financial arrangements	Neighborhood Housing Service	—
Property conveyance signed (clear title)	City	—
Complete rehabilitation	Homesteader/contractor	—
Code approval	Appropriate city departments	—
Occupy property	Homesteader	—
Complete occupancy requirements	Homesteader	2 years after occupancy

Source: Compiled by the authors.

TABLE 5.22

Pittsburgh, Pennsylvania City Path

Event	Actor	Time
Selection of properties	Real Estate Division	—
Advertisement of properties	Real Estate Division	—
Rehabilitation analysis (work write-up costs)	Urban Redevelopment Authority/Neighborhood Housing Service	—
Certification of homesteader	Housing coordinator	—
Transferral of property (sale)	Real Estate Division	—
Title transfer	City	—

Source: Compiled by the authors.

The fact that 48 houses were taken into the program in one year without cost to the city is a measurable benefit. These 48 houses will become tax producing in 1977.

Questionnaire schedules from Pittsburgh homesteaders indicate that homesteaders perceive considerable benefit from homesteading both to the city and to themselves. All those surveyed said they would not have owned a home otherwise. They said this was their first home to own. They perceived heightened neighborhood interest. However, the opportunity to own a home of their own was considered the most important benefit. Homesteaders said they would recommend the program to other cities and other citizens. One recommendation to other citizens says, "Start as soon as you can. It really makes you feel like you belong to a place."

ROCKFORD, ILLINOIS

Background

Several Rockford city officials went to Washington in March of 1974, immediately after the city council had voted to approve a homesteading ordinance.[34] As a result of their meeting with H.R. Crawford, assistant secretary of HUD, Rockford was designated a Federal Urban Homesteading Pilot City. Fifty abandoned houses in Rockford were authorized as part of its pilot project. In April 1974, the Urban Homestead Board began to develop criteria for the execution of the program. Their goal was "to rehabilitate neighborhoods through home occupancy"[35] and to "improve the quality of housing in accordance with the homestead program."[36]

Since that time 22 houses have been awarded as homesteads, 10 in an initial lottery on August 5, 1974 and 12 in a second lottery held on March 21, 1975. The average homestead is 40 years old. One homestead family reported repair costs estimated at $3,700 but expected to do much of the work themselves.[37]

Approximately 700 applications were mailed in response to the first offering of properties. Of this number, 150 returned the preliminary applications for lottery number one and, later, 137 returned applications for lottery number two. Some applicants were rejected because they did not fulfill the residency requirement. (According to the report, Urban Homesteading in Rockford, an applicant must live within the corporate limits of the city of Rockford.) Some others were eliminated after interviews because they failed to meet other criteria. Others withdrew on their own, leaving 41 applicants for the first 10 houses and 45 applicants for the second group of 12 who met the requirements of the program. Rockford officials decided to use a lottery for the final selection of homesteaders.

Twenty-two questionnaire schedules were mailed to Rockford for distribution to homesteaders. Four of these were completed and returned. Two civic-leader forms were also returned.

Unique Characteristics

Rockford, Illinois has many counterparts in the American midwest. There are other cities of similar size and age and with similar housing problems. Why has Rockford pursued homesteading as one answer to its housing needs? We find that in many of the cities that have undertaken homesteading, much of the impetus came from a single person. This is true in Rockford as well. The name of Alderman Michael J. O'Neal is closely associated with the homesteading project. Mr. O'Neal serves ex officio on the homestead board. In that capacity he continues to guide and strengthen the program.

Otherwise, Rockford can be considered a prime area for homesteading because it owns a large number of unoccupied, deteriorated or deteriorating or economically unproductive houses and was unable to attract private developers to these sites. For this reason, the homestead board was empowered to hold or to obtain real property through gifts or by other legal processes.

Laws and Administration

The City Council of Rockford voted to approve a proposed Urban Homestead Ordinance on February 25, 1974.[38] An amendment to that ordinance created a homestead board in April of that same year.[39] Rockford's home-rule charter provides that the city may hold, manage, and dispose of property. This type of charter obviates the need for state enabling legislation.

The homestead board is appointed by the mayor to administer the homestead program and to serve no more than two three-year terms without compensation.

The city assumes the duty of keeping a catalog of all unoccupied dwellings and vacant lots within the city. The homestead board selects parcels from this list that it deems appropriate for rehabilitation or new construction. The city then deeds these selected sites to the board for disposition. Although the board is empowered to obtain real property through gifts or by other legal processes, it is denied the right of condemnation. Their other duties and responsibilities include acquisition of property and implementation of the program.

The homestead board hires a professional staff of its own and also uses other relevant city agencies.

The homesteader must meet certain minimum requirements as established by the homestead board. Rehabilitation and/or construction is allowed.

An additional criterion has been established by the homestead board. Although the program is open to all people regardless of their income, the applicant must have sufficient funds or the borrowing ability to repair the homestead site. The program is not attempting to provide housing for low-income people but to rehabilitate neighborhoods through home occupancy.

Financial Options

Loan funds are provided by commercial institutions to the homestead board. The loans are made by the board to the homesteader at the current commercial rate. The Central National Bank provided $50,000 at 9 1/2 percent for the rehabilitation of the houses in the first lottery. The second lottery is financed by a loan fund of $70,000 from the Rock River Savings and Loan. Under the lease-purchase agreement, the homestead board retains title to the property until the four-year occupancy clause is fulfilled. This enables the board to procure conventional loan money on its own cognizance. Since the homesteader does not obtain the title until he has fulfilled all the requirements, he would be unable to borrow the money without the deed from a conventional source. Although the homesteader believes his is a local agency loan or a Rockford Homestead Board loan, the financing is not done by the city from its own funds but is actually arranged by the homestead board through conventional establishments.

Support Services

There are several community services available to a Rockford homesteader. The board counseling begins with the initial interview. At that time, the financial status of the applicant is verified so that his ability to pay the costs of the rehabilitation or to carry a loan is assured. Financial counseling and the availability of loan funds through the board is a major service of the Rockford Homestead Board.

Rockford provides technical services, also. A work-up sheet which describes the necessary repairs to the home is revised at the time of the initial interview, also. This enables the applicant to know

exactly what he is undertaking. He is then able to make decisions
regarding what portions of the work he can do himself and what
portions must be contracted out. The regular inspection schedule
by various city departments ensures adherence to a work-priority
schedule and may simplify the work organization for the homesteader.
A tool library is provided for use by the homesteader. Cooperative
purchasing of building supplies and contractors' services is encouraged. The community renewal staff conducts the personal interviews
with the homesteaders and counsels each applicant regarding the
repair and rehabilitation work.

Benefits

Rockford citizen leaders and officials believe that homesteading
is a benefit to the city. They stress the improved appearance of
the city and the fact that homesteading discourages vandalism. Some
citizens itemized the benefits to private businesses, such as to
contractors and to heating, plumbing, and electrical suppliers.
Improved business can also be considered a benefit to the city.
According to these citizens, homeowners other than homesteaders
have been encouraged by the homesteading program to improve and
maintain their homes. This, they believe, discourages further
abandonment and deterioration. In this way homesteading has been
a catalyst that encourages neighborhood stability. One Rockford
executive recommends an acceleration of the existing program.

All the homesteaders interviewed and all other citizens responding
indicated that they would recommend homesteading to other citizens
and other cities.

In terms of its goal, "to rehabilitate neighborhoods," officials
see homesteading as "one of several 'tools' that can be used to preserve and encourage neighborhood rehabilitation efforts. It can be an
effective method that will assist in stopping the serious decay that is
affecting our urban cores."[40]

All homesteaders responded that they were satisfied with the
program "a great deal." According to the questionnaire survey,
75 percent of the homesteaders would not have been able to own a
home in any other way. Homeownership, then, is a major benefit.
The homesteader profile published by the city of Rockford describes
all homesteaders as "renters" previously.[41] Being able to provide a
home for their families was considered the greatest benefit of the
homestead program. This enhanced their own satisfaction as well
as their satisfaction with the city. Every homesteader agreed that the
program should be expanded, and all said they would recommend
it to other cities and other citizens.

TABLE 5.23

Comparative Data for Rockford

City[a]		Homesteader	
Population	147,370	Number of homesteader responses	4
Average family income	$12,085	Average income	$7,500
Total housing units	51,376	Number of homesteads	22
Percent substandard units	3%	Rehabilitation (average costs)	$5,350
Percent overcrowded units	6%	Average family size	2-3
Median value of housing	$19,300	Median age[b]	27 years
Units over 30 years old	44%	Average age of homestead parcel	40 years

[a]U.S. Bureau of the Census, 1970.
[b]Rockford Department of Community Renewal, "Urban Homesteading,"
p. 8.
Source: Compiled by the authors.

TABLE 5.24

Rockford, Illinois Homesteader Path

Event	Actor	Time
Application filed	Homesteader	—
Interview held	Dept. of Community Renewal/Homesteader	—
Property conveyance signed (lease-purchase agreement)	Homestead Board/Homesteader	—
Financial arrangements (conventional loan)	Homestead Board	—
Major rehabilitation	Homesteader/Contractor	—
Inspections	Appropriate city departments	—
Code approval	Appropriate city departments	—
Occupy property	Homesteader	18 months from conveyance
Complete rehabilitation	Homesteader	—
Complete occupancy requirements	Homesteader	48 months from conveyance
Acquire clear title	Homestead Board	48 months from conveyance

Source: Compiled by the authors.

TABLE 5.25

Rockford, Illinois City Path

Event	Actor	Time
Selection of properties	Homestead Board	—
Rehabilitation analysis	Dept. of Community Renewal	—
Advertisement of properties	Homestead Board	—
Transferral of property (lottery)	Homestead Board	—
Property conveyance (lease-purchase agreement)	Homestead Board	—
Inspection of work	Appropriate city departments	18 months after transferral
Title transfer	City	48 months after transferral

Source: Compiled by the authors.

ST. LOUIS, MISSOURI

Background

In the late 1960s St. Louis began having serious problems in real-estate-tax collection. White flight to the suburbs aggravated the situation. Between 1960 and 1970, 12.8 percent of the total housing units were lost (destroyed, changed in use, deteriorated).[42] In 1971 the Missouri legislature passed the Land Reutilization Act.[43] This shortened the foreclosure procedure on abandoned properties and enabled cities to take title by bidding at public auction at a set price. (Formerly, it was almost a three-year process.) Also in 1971 a St. Louis law created a city Land Reutilization Authority (LRA) to acquire and manage these properties.[44] Urban homesteading was then possible. It was implemented in January 1974, with LRA administering it. At present it is considered a purely administrative program that is run as a real-estate business. There are no legal requirements other than initial city acquisition of property and minimum sale price to homesteaders.

The goals of the St. Louis program are to return properties to the tax rolls and to have them occupied by "stable" residents. No financial aid is offered. This should ensure that the buyers will be financially secure. The data cited in Table 27 indicate that the city of St. Louis has a fairly nontransient, moderate-income population with a high number of derelict buildings. These are among the factors that led to the goal formulation of maintaining financial stability and mainstream middle-class values in the city by attracting middle-income families into the city.

An attempt to broaden the goals to include housing opportunities for the poor was made by two Democratic alderpersons. The houses would sell for one dollar. The proposal would have offered city-funded and guaranteed loans at 3 percent interest, tax deductible. The rehabilitation period would be three years with no property taxes. This proposal, however, was strongly opposed.[45]

The city acquires its houses at public auction. The 1971 state law made possible a procedure that combines foreclosure action on the tax liens and quiets title against all claims. This results in a reduction in costs and time for processing the property. In addition, several pieces of property can be grouped into one suit for legal services. The costs are approximately $50 for each parcel.[46] The LRA pays a set amount for the properties that is equal to delinquent taxes plus interest and penalty fees. Private buyers must bid over them. The time period from delinquent real-estate taxes to sheriff's sale is at least eight months. The sheriff sends to LRA a list of properties bought for confirmation of sale. The properties are then appraised. Deeds are recorded 30 days after confirmation of the sale.

The LRA may then place these in a land bank, give properties to other governmental bodies to be used for public purposes, or sell them to homesteaders for no less than two-thirds of their appraised price or less than $100. Prices range from $400 to $1,200.[47] The results have been remarkable: "The net effect of this law in the City of St. Louis has been a rise in real estate tax collections from 90% to 99%."[48]

Although there is provision for negotiation on the sale price of the property to the homesteader, the buyer must prove sufficient financial abilities to succeed in the program. Mr. Backers explains, "We're not running a social service. We're in the real estate business, and we want our customers to succeed. We do job and credit checks on each prospect, and advise the banks regarding restoration loans."[49]

After rehabilitation is completed and certified by the city inspections department, the homesteader who has leased has an option to purchase the property. According to the lease-purchase agreement, 90 percent of the lease payment applies to the purchase. By the end of 1974, between 175 and 200 homes had been purchased on lease and 75 homes had been purchased outright with cash.[50]

There were 300 homesteaders as of July 1975. Seventy homesteader questionnaire schedules were sent. There were 28 returned of which 26 were complete. A homesteader-official questionnaire and two civic-leader questionnaires were also returned.

Unique Characteristics

Founded in 1764, St. Louis was incorporated as a city in 1822. The city's abandoned houses have increased rapidly in the last 15 years. Those included in the homestead program have been scattered, in viable neighborhoods. The more seriously blighted areas are on the north side. The homes that are chosen are all below code but structurally sound. Some are historic; most are single family.[51] Backers foresees a possible 500 houses in the program by 1979. There are presently 300. Although there are thousands of derelict buildings on the delinquent tax rolls, Backers projects that only about 2,000 would be suitable for homesteading.[52]

Laws and Administration

In correspondence from Mr. Backers on the details of the program, he emphasized that the program is kept simple with no legal mechanisms. There are no support services or financial arrangements.

There has been minimal advertisement, but annual house tours have attracted many potential buyers. The program operates as follows:

1. City gains title at public auction.
2. LRA evaluates condition and location. If it is in a viable neighborhood or in a neighborhood scheduled for community improvement, it is made available for homesteading. Otherwise, it is placed in a land bank.
3. LRA determines sale price (market value before restoration).
4. Properties are described in a real estate book for potential homesteaders to view.
5. Homesteader qualifications: (flexible)
    a. Be financially able to rehabilitate and maintain house at contracted standards.
    b. Agree to improve property to meet code requirements.
    c. Be a normal family of 1 man and 1 woman plus children, if any.
    d. Have good moral character.
    e. Agree to occupy for 3 years after acquiring title.
6. Homesteader has a lease with option to buy after restoration is completed.
7. The title is granted upon completion and payment in full of purchase price (by down payment and monthly payments).
8. Property is tax exempt until 1 year after transfer of title.[53]

The homesteaders are selected according to ability to meet the financial obligations incurred. The houses are selected according to condition, possible resale value, and neighborhood viability. These factors emphasize the importance of a financial success for the city and for the homesteader.

Of the 15 homesteaders who recorded their take-home pay, eight received under $10,000 a year. Those over $10,000 have two or more wage earners in the household. Half the homesteaders are married. Prior to becoming a homesteader, 50 percent paid rent of less than $100. Usually this did not include utilities. Before becoming homesteaders, 83 percent lived in the city. There were 38 percent who previously owned a home. Many St. Louis homesteaders appear to be lower-income renters who resided within the city.

TABLE 5.26

Comparative Data for St. Louis

City*		Homesteader	
Population	750,000	Number of homesteader responses	26
Median income	$7,500	Median income	$7,500
Units over 30 years old	80%	Percent black	54%
		Average age Under 30 years old	46%
		Over 40 years old	46%
		Number of homesteads	300

*U.S. Bureau of the Census, 1970.
Source: Compiled by the authors.

TABLE 5.27

St. Louis, Missouri Homesteader Path

Event	Actor	Time
Application	Homesteader	—
Interview	Homesteader/LRA	—
Property conveyance (sale, buy, or lease-purchase)	LRA	—
Financial arrangement	Conventional-personal savings	—
Major rehabilitation	Homesteader/Contractor	—
Inspections—Approval for occuparcy	Inspections Dept.	—
Occupy property	Homesteader	—
Complete rehabilitation	Homesteader/Contractor	2 years from conveyance
Acquire clear title	Homesteader/City	after rehabilitation completion and payment
Taxes	Homesteader	1 year after title
Complete occupancy	Homesteader	3 years after title

Source: Compiled by the authors.

TABLE 5.28

St. Louis, Missouri City Path

Rehabilitation analysis of property	LRA	8 months to 1 year after sheriff's sale
Selection of properties	LRA	9 months to 1 year after sheriff's sale
Certification of homesteaders	LRA	—
Advertisement of properties	LRA (real-estate book)	—
Transferral of property to homesteader (auction)	LRA	—
Property conveyance (title or lease-purchase agreement)	LRA	At sale
Inspection	Inspections Dept.	2 years from sale
Title transferral	LRA	After rehabilitation and payment for house

Source: Compiled by the authors.

Benefits

Civic-leader responses were divided. One cited homesteading benefits of bringing middle-income persons into the city and of improving the city tax base. The other viewed the program as one that could potentially affect neighborhoods. Private investment was viewed as a more effective tool for improving the city. He saw the program as a means of stabilizing real-estate values and of affecting sales and rentals of houses.

The most frequently mentioned benefit in the homesteader-questionnaire responses is an inexpensive house. This indicates that they felt a need for housing and for a sound investment. The flexibility of the program is a benefit to one homesteader. Another was interested in settling in a low income neighborhood.

In response to a question on "unexpected benefits," an official stated that for every homestead house sold, ten others are sold in the private sector. This is apparently referring to other houses in the area or perhaps a general rise in inner-city real-estate sales. In either case, the homesteading took place prior to, and perhaps led to, the increased private-sector sales.

WASHINGTON, D.C.

On May 31, 1975 the authors met with the two Washington urban-homesteading counselors, Messrs. Brooks and Moore. They explained the details of their portion of the program and gave us a tour of homes in progress. There are many parts of the program, however that remain unclear, particularly the administrative structure. The majority of our time in Washington was spent in unaccompanied on-site observation of the program. Although the Washington program had received considerable mention by the media, there was no information (published or unpublished) available. The visit was essential to gather data and to view this unique administration.

Background

In 1974 congressional legislation established an urban-homesteading program in the District of Columbia with two classes of property available: land acquired by the district government through tax foreclosures, and property owned by HUD. [54]

One of the early proponents of urban homesteading was Nadine Winter, now councilperson in Washington, D.C. She is also on the board of directors for Hospitality House, Inc., a community center.

Hospitality House and the Office of Housing and Community Development are cosponsors of the program.

The first 13 houses were awarded in July 1974. Conditional titles were granted in December 1974. Seed money, the initial funds used to develop a project, was obtained from businesses in the area so that a quasi-public corporation could be established for rehabilitation loans. Some cities have gathered seed money from several sources to establish a revolving loan fund. The board of directors of Hospitality House makes all major decisions and selects the homesteaders.

The goals of the program have been to stabilize blighted neighborhoods and to have everyone—city, neighborhood, contractor, buyer—benefit. The houses, all of which were owned by HUD, had been abandoned and boarded up. The program will use any parcels regardless of condition as homesteads.

The houses are scattered throughout northeast and northwest Washington where there are many abandoned buildings. We observed many in well-kept moderate-income neighborhoods.

Unique Characteristics

The city is quite old; L'Enfant laid out the city plan in 1791. Its ordered early growth helped to ensure some spaciousness, even in presently blighted neighborhoods. The recycling of these houses through homesteading has had "the strong support of some powerful individuals" in the one-year-old local government. (Unsolicited comment of a homesteader on a returned questionnaire.)

Councilwoman Winter remains the principal mentor of the program to the staff as well as the homesteaders. Her leadership is a unique characteristic in the Washington program.

Another unique characteristic of the program is its scope. It appears to operate as a neighborhood project from a neighborhood center rather than as a citywide housing program.

Laws and Administration

The city council voted to initiate and support this program. It is authorized to allocate funds to the corporation. This organization, the District of Columbia Development Corporation, has $160,000 as seed money. Urban homesteading operates as a separate agency, responsible to Hospitality House. Two counselors handle the support services; one is a housing counselor, the other a construction advisor.

There are no code allowances. New code standards must be met if, for instance, new plumbing is installed. The houses are "sold" for

one dollar. The buyers are given one year to bring houses up to
city code. If the work is contracted out, it should be completed in
90 days. The buyer receives a conditional title intially. After the
rehabilitation is completed or has attained a level of safety, occupancy begins. A five-year period of residency is required.

Homesteaders must have been residents of Washington, D.C. for
at least one year. The family size is matched with available houses.
Consideration is given to income and capability of maintaining the
house. The income level for the program is not fixed, but it is not
for the poor, according to Mr. Moore. The major criterion is capability. This is determined by prior records, credits, and personal
observation.

There were 13 homesteaders as of July 1975. Responses to the
survey included five homesteaders, a homesteading official, and two
civic leaders. The homesteader questionnaires were distributed by
Barbara Carter of the city's Office of Housing and Community
Development.

The houses presently in the program were acquired from HUD.
Moore indicated that the growth of the program depends upon the
number of houses HUD makes available. Taxes on the abandoned
houses become payable upon sale by the city. The assessment is
usually quite low, around $13,000, although the resale values go up
to $60,000 or $70,000. [55] All houses offered by HUD are used. The
program is scheduled to continue with 13 to 20 additional houses a
year.

Financial Options

In addition to the loans available from the D.C. Development
Corporation for up to $17,000, commercial loan institutions provide
loans. The Development Corporation interest rates are 10 percent
for 20-year loans. The legislation also includes an authorization to
guarantee a loan or advance money if an applicant cannot obtain
financing elsewhere.

Support Services

Once the quasipublic corporation was established, the program's
success depended upon support services. These are seen by the
counselors as vital to the homesteaders. The services provided are
comprehensive: financial counseling for a loan and for personal
budgeting, personal counseling, construction adviser, award to low
bidder for contract work, homeownership orientation, and insurance

counseling. These are designed to prevent shoddy work by the contractors and "rip-offs" to the homesteaders as well as to ensure that
each homesteader will be a success. The homesteader selects the
materials to be used. The contractor must sign an agreement before-
hand to meet certain standards. Loans from the corporation may only
go to $17,500. The contractor must agree to that price no matter the
extent of the deterioration. Moore claims this is possible because of
the current recession in the housing industry.

The services offered by the urban homesteading staff include group
lectures and individual counseling. In addition, neighborhood groups
are formed—block clubs—to assimilate the newcomers and to encourage
other residents to renovate their own houses. These are organized
by the staff.

Benefits

Civic leaders questioned in the city gave a high appraisal of the
program. Both said that real-estate values had been raised in affected neighborhoods, that the city is benefiting financially by improving the tax base but especially socially and cosmetically. Specifically, urban homesteading helps meet the housing needs, provides
opportunities for citizens and improves their attitudes, and improves
neighborhood stability. They agreed that the appearance of the city
is improved. One said that vandalism is discouraged. Both felt that
certain businesses had been affected, such as construction and
home-repair firms. Also small "mom and pop" stores were mentioned as benefiting from the program. One respondent sums up this
optimistic view with: "[Urban homesteading] raised confidence of
those who believe in urban life."

It would seem that the city is reaching its goal of stabilizing
blighted neighborhoods, although the final judgment cannot be made
for several years. The other goal of "benefiting everyone" does not
refer to a particular income group. It has intentionally been operating
with persons above low income. One civic leader suggested a change
in the program so that local low-interest rehabilitation loans could
be provided without regard to income.

Homesteader response was very enthusiastic. Of the 12 questionnaires sent to the city, 4 were completed and returned. All spot-
lighted the support services and staff as especially helpful. They
also recommended an expansion of the program to include more
houses. The income level as measured by take-home pay of participants here is middle class. Three of the four said they would have
attempted to buy a home even without homesteading. None of these
however had owned a home previously. The fourth respondent had

TABLE 5.29

Comparative Data for Washington

City		Homesteader	
Population	756,000	Number of home-steader responses	4
Median income	$9,583	Median income	$13,000
Units over 30 years old	47%	Number black	4
Median housing value	$21,300	Median housing assess-ment (before rehabili-tation)	$13,000
Number of persons per room	2.7	Median rehabilitation costs	$17,500
		Number of homesteads	13

Source: Compiled by the authors.

TABLE 5.30

Washington, D.C. Homesteader Path

Event	Actor	Time
Application	Homesteader	—
Property conveyance (interview/conditional title)	Hospitality House	—
Taxes	Homesteader	Immediately
Financial arrangements	D.C. Development Corp. or conventional loan	—
Rehabilitation	Homesteader	1 year
	Contractor	90 days
Inspections and approval for occupancy	City	After safety level reached or rehabilitation complete
Occupy property	Homesteader	Same
Complete occupancy requirement	Homesteader	5 years from of occupancy

Source: Compiled by the authors.

TABLE 5.31

Washington, D.C. City Path

Event	Actor	Time
Selection of properties	HUD	—
Advertisement of properties	DHCD*	—
Rehabilitation analysis of properties	DHCD	—
Certification of homesteaders	Hospitality House	—
Transferral of property to homesteader (interview)	Hospitality House	—
Property conveyance	City	—
Inspections for completed rehabilitation	City	1 year/ sweat equity 90 days/contractor
Support services	Urban-homestead staff	Throughout 5-year homestead period

*Department of Housing and Community Development.
Source: Compiled by the authors.

owned a home, had a bad experience with it, and would not consider
the financial investment again without homesteading. The take-home
pay ranges from $6,000 to $17,000, with the median at $13,000 a
year. Their skills are limited, generally, to maintenance of the
property rather than specific restoration skills. All of these contracted out the rehabilitation work. The homesteaders are all black,
married, over 30 years old, and have several children. They all
expressed appreciation for the opportunity to own a home provided
through this program.

WILMINGTON, DELAWARE

The authors visited Wilmington, Delaware for on-site inspection
and personal interviews on June 4, 1975. Mr. Theodore Spaulding
conducted us on a complete tour of all homesteading neighborhoods.
A firsthand knowledge of Wilmington, the first homesteading city in
the United States, seemed essential for a complete study.

Background

The inauguration of homesteading in Wilmington was reported in
many of the major mewspapers, magazines, and trade journals. The
New York Times, Washington Post, Wall Street Journal, and many
other newspapers responded to the one dollar homes with extensive
articles and human-interest stories. Daniel Frawley, the first homesteader in Wilmington, was pictured with his winning lottery number,
interviewed, and profiled. Wilmington received 300 letters of inquiry
from other cities immediately following this extensive press coverage.
Although many of the articles were highly optimistic, several writers
expressed doubts about the legal entanglements and the financial
difficulties. Gail Bronson, writing in the Wall Street Journal, was
one of the skeptics. Unless there is public subsidy of the rehabilitation, the homesteader would be "led into a bad deal," said Bronson.[56]
Nevertheless, the action of the Wilmington City Council on May 27,
1973, which created the first urban homestead ordinance in the United
States, engendered high expectations among officials and citizens alike.
As predicted, Wilmington has encountered legal and financial restraints. The enactments and the program that has resulted have helped
many other cities plan their programs carefully and avoid some of
the pitfalls.
Section 3 of the Wilmington homestead ordinance states the goal:
"to improve the quality of housing."[57] Mayor Maloney has been quoted
in many press releases as he amplified the city's dilemma. "We have

over 2,000 abandoned, dilapidated houses in Wilmington that produce
no tax revenue and that blight the surrounding neighborhoods. Why
not give them away?" Converting tax liabilities into tax-producing
units became the second goal of Wilmington's program.

Although Wilmington has a stock of 2,000 abandoned and deteriorated houses, only 96 of these are owned by the city. These 96
were acquired by sheriff's sale for back taxes. Of these houses, 78
were deemed fit for homesteading. Thirty are now in the program.
The city recently enacted two ordinances to speed the process of
acquisition. The ordinances give the Department of Licenses and
Inspections the authority to either rehabilitate or demolish such units.
It is anticipated that about 36 houses each year will be acquired this
way. This may mean that there will be about 18 houses each year
available for homesteading. Previous experience indicates about
50 percent of such houses are not feasible for homesteading. To
increase the available stock Wilmington has petitioned HUD for per-
mission to use properties acquired in urban-renewal areas.

Twenty-seven houses have been awarded to homestead applicants
since the program was inaugurated. There were 300 people who
applied for the first available group of houses. The applications
came from Wilmington, from nearby cities, and even from out of
state. Residents of the homestead neighborhood rarely qualify as
homesteaders, according to the program's director, Theodore
Spaulding. He says this is because the areas where homestead sites
are located do not often include people who can afford to repair them.[58]
The homestead sites are scattered in several neighborhoods. A neighborhood qualifies for homesteading if it is less than 25 percent abandoned.

Because several people qualified as applicants for each house, a
lottery system has been used to select the homesteaders. Eight
houses are now occupied. The remaining parcels are in various
stages of rehabilitation. The homestead properties have been assessed
at $5,500 on the average, prior to renovation. The average homestead
is described as a three-bedroom brick house, and the average rehabilitation cost is about $7,000 if the work is contracted out. Many home-
steaders have been able to rehabilitate for far less with the help of
friends, church groups, and various other community organizations.

Five homesteader forms were left in Wilmington during the on-site
inspection in June 1975. Four of these forms have been returned. These
data vary considerably from the report in the Wilmington in-house
publication, Wilmington Homestead Program, as seen in Table 5.32.

Unique Characteristics

Wilmington is an old and historic city. Until very recently, the housing code required double masonry construction. [59] This has resulted in an abundance of very old, structurally sound buildings. Many of these are small row houses which can be rehabilitated for relatively modest amounts. According to Dee Wedemeyer, writing in the Nation's Cities, Wilmington had a population decline of 30,000 in 20 years; 1 in 15 houses is vacant. [60] These are all facts that created the climate for homesteading. The program is small and experimental and expects to continue this way.

Laws and Administration

Wilmington passed a city ordinance that enacted the homestead program and created a homestead board on May 27, 1973. No special or enabling state legislation was required. The homestead board originally consisted of five members. This was subsequently increased to seven by amendment to the ordinance. The board consists of six city officials and one citizen (a banker or building-and-loan executive). All serve as volunteers. They include the following: director of planning and development; director of urban renewal; commissioner of licenses and inspections; commissioner of public works; assistant city solicitor; mayor's public policy assistant; citizen representative.

The board is empowered to make policy decisions, identify properties, qualify the homesteaders, and provide technical assistance to them. The professional staff consists of four full-time personnel. The annual administrative expense is $70,000. The administration coordinates three disparate elements in the city: the Wilmington Homestead Board, the Wilmington City Housing Corporation, and conventional lenders.

Homesteaders are qualified according to criteria established in the ordinance plus additional qualifications established by the homestead board. An attempt is made to match the size of the applicants' household with the size of the chosen property. There are no minimum or maximum income levels. The Wilmington board's affirmative-action statement adds flexibility to the ordinance: It disavows discrimination on the basis of age, sex, race, color, creed, or national origin. It stresses the technical-assistance support system designed to ensure participation of low- and middle-income groups.

Financial Options

In Wilmington, financing the rehabilitation of a homestead can be approached in two ways. The homesteader can apply for private financing from a conventional loan institution, or the homesteader can participate in a homestead loan program sponsored by the Wilmington City Housing Corporation (WCHC) under Resolution 74-137. Passed by the city council on July 11, 1974, the WCHC provides a 40-percent loan guarantee. This guarantee enables the banks to give special consideration to homesteaders who might not otherwise qualify for loans. The terms are 8 1/2 percent with 15-year loans on amounts up to $10,000 and 10-year loans for less than $6,500.

One serious financial problem was overcome in May 1974. The homestead ordinance, in granting a conditional deed, specified that a parcel would revert to the city if a homesteader defaulted on any of the specified conditions. This impaired the homesteaders' ability to secure financing. Accordingly, the ordinance was amended (Ord. 74-030) to allow the lending institutions to secure first lien on the property.[61] The conventional lending institutions are now willing to lend long-term mortgage money.

Tax assistance has been provided under Ordinance 72-081.[62] This provision grants partial tax exemption for improvements to existing structures. The ordinance states "that the improved property will be exempt from real estate taxation to the extent of 150% of the increase in assessed valuation attributable to the new construction." This is computed in the following manner. If a house is assessed at $10,000, and $12,000 is spent on rehabilitation, half of $12,000, or $6,000 is deducted from the assessed value for tax purposes. The homesteader would than pay taxes on the basis of $4,000. This tax-incentive program has a life span of five years.

Support Services

The city of Wilmington has provided legal, financial, and technical counseling for homesteaders. A grant from a private foundation supports half-salaries of two employees, a full-time rehabilitation counselor, and a financial/budget counselor.

Once an applicant qualifies as a homesteader, a "buddy" system is established whereby each homesteader is paired off with a member of the homestead board. The board member provides direct personalized assistance throughout the three-year period of homesteading. The board member assists the homesteader to finalize the rehabilitation plans and specifications; secure three certified bids for all subcontract work; secure rehabilitation financing; and monitor work progress. The board member also provides additional supportive services as required.

A monthly meeting between the homestead board and all homesteaders has been in effect since the program's inception.

The Department of Licenses and Inspections provides a progress chart which enables the homesteader to establish rehabilitation priorities. This chart lists each code violation and notes beside each item a time limitation for repairs.

The city of Wilmington has taken steps to obtain additional services from other public and private sources:

1. A tool lending library.
2. Home-improvement training program.
3. Free architectural services.
4. Family counseling; homemaker service; money management.
5. Volunteer labor support.

Benefits

In his testimony before a congressional committee, Mayor Thomas Maloney itemized many benefits that have accrued to the city as a result of homesteading. [63] He stressed the results of the volunteer rehabilitation program. He told of high-school students who helped in homestead rehabilitation, an activity that he said rekindled their interest in the city and improved their school performance. He made note of people in a drug program who had participated in a similar fashion. A senior-citizen program of the same nature is in the offing, he said.

Seven potential benefits of urban homesteading are listed in The Wilmington Homestead Program. This has been entered in the Congressional Record. These benefits cannot be tested because the program has not functioned long enough to assess its impact empirically:

1. Offer homeownership to those who could not otherwise afford their own homes. (The homestead survey which was conducted for this report provides some data that could be used to measure this variable; i.e., 50% of Wilmington homesteaders responding to the survey said they would not have attempted to buy a home without the Homestead Program.)

2. Revitalize deteriorated neighborhoods by increasing
   their economic viability.
3. Convert tax liabilities into tax producing units.
4. Reduce crime.
5. Promote economic and racial integration (100% of
   homesteaders surveyed for this report indicated
   that there was "more integration in this neighborhood" than their former one).
6. Create a new force in the community to demand
   quality municipal services.
7. Provide lower income homesteaders with training
   which may lead to new job skills.[64]

The respondent who completed the official questionnaire for this study comments, "Neighborhood homes generally begin to improve to update with homesteaders. Homestead areas are developing at a steady pace."

The principal benefits that homesteaders cited had accrued to them were homeownership, development of new skills, increase in property values, and involvement in community life.

All the homesteaders responding to the survey indicated they would recommend homesteading to other cities and other citizens. One homesteader qualified this recommendation to cities under 1,000,000 population. "Smaller cities experience less radical elements of blight, white flight, plus having a more personal rela-tionship with city officials to get things accomplished sooner."

TABLE 5.32

Comparative Data for Wilmington

City[a]		Homesteader[b]	Survey Data	City Data
Population	80,386	Number of homesteader responses	4	
Percent black	43.6%	Percent black	25%	75%
Total housing units	29,971	Number of homesteads	27	
Mean income	$9,826	Average income	$18,000	$9,200
Percent overcrowded units	6%	Average size family	2.1	4
Median housing value	$11,000	Average assessment		$5,500
Percent units over 30 years old	72%	Average rehabilitation costs		$7,000

[a] U.S. Bureau of the Census, 1970.

[b] Differential is due to different populations surveyed. The survey data was based on four out of five occupied homesteads. City data was based on the total number in the program. Differences may be due to the fact that those who complete rehabilitation and move in quickly are likely to be those who contract out the work, that is, the upper-income group.

Source: Compiled by the authors.

TABLE 5.33

Wilmington, Delaware Homesteader Path

Event	Actor	Time
Application filed	Homesteader	—
Interview held	Homestead/representative of Homestead Board	—
Property conveyance signed (conditional deed)	Homesteader/city	—
Financial arrangements (conventional or WCHC)	Homesteader	—
Select contractor	Homesteader	—
Inspections	Dept. of Licenses and Inspections	—
Approval for occupancy	Dept. of Code	18 months after conveyance
Occupy property	Homesteader	18 months after conveyance
Complete rehabilitation	Homesteader	
Complete occupancy requirement	Homesteader	36 months after conveyance
Acquire clear title	Homesteader/city	36 months after conveyance

Source: Compiled by the authors.

TABLE 5.34

Wilmington, Delaware City Path

Event	Actor	Time
Selection of properties	Homestead board	—
Rehabilitation analysis	Dept. of Licenses and Inspection	—
Advertisement of Properties	Homestead Board	—
Certification of Homesteader	Homestead Board	42 days after advertisement
Transferral of property (conditional deed)	City council/mayor	—
Work write-up (code violations)	Dept. of Licenses and Inspections	—
Inspection	Dept. of Licenses and Inspections	18 months after transferral
Title transfer (fee simple)	City clerk	36 months after transferral

Source: Compiled by the authors.

TABLE 5.35

Comparison of City Program Structure

	Unique Characteristics	Adoption	Administration
Baltimore	Historic area; umbrella agency for all homeownership programs	Resolution adopted by Board of Estimates in 1973	Home Ownership Development Program staff of seven, under Dept. of Housing and Community Dev.; $120,000 annual budget; $1,000 per unit
Buffalo	Frame stock difficult to use; vacant land used	Ordinance 1974	Dept. of Community Development, four part-time staff
Camden	Large number of aged and abandoned units; permissive N.J. statutes	Ordinance 1974	Real Estate Board of nine members, staff of three members
Dayton	Coalition of political and civic leaders for rehabilitation	Administrative decision of city-wide Development Corporation 1973	City-Wide Development Corporation
Minneapolis	State enabling legislation for city bonds; nonprofit corp. can acquire house	State legislature; permissive legislation 1974; administrative procedure adopted Dec. 1974	Steering committee of citizens, community groups, public officials; Housing and Redev. Auth.; $2,500 per unit
Newark	Large stock of abandoned houses; permissive N.J. statutes	1974	Dept. of Tax Collection
Philadelphia	Unique architecture; city funds for acquisition and rehabilitation; public/private venture; environment criteria for site selection; homesteaders selected by need	Ordinance July 1973, amended Feb. 1975	Homestead Board of 11 appointed by mayor, nine citizens, staff of 11; $219,000 annual budget
Pittsburgh	Two sources of homes, administered differently	Exec. decision of mayor, Nov. 1973	Real Estate Div. of Dept. of Lands and Bldgs., also Urban Redevelopment Authority
Rockford	Vacant-land option; total private funding	Ordinance Feb. 1974, amended April 1974	Homestead Board appointed by mayor, hires staff, uses other city agencies
St. Louis	Historic area; state law quiets all claims; total private funding	Administrative decision of Land Reutilization Authority 1973	Land Reutilization Authority
Washington	Public/private venture, D.C. Dev. Corp. with $160,000 seed money	Congressional enabling legislation 1974; city council vote to initiate and support	Hospitality House (neighborhood facility) staff of two from city administer from Hospitality House
Wilmington	First operating program; vacant-land option	Ordinance May 1973.	Homestead Board of six city officials and one banker; staff of four; $7,000 annual budget; $1,500 per unit

Source: Compiled by the authors.

TABLE 5.36

Comparison of Abandoned Housing Conditions

	Source	Abandoned Stock	Units Suitable for Homesteading
Baltimore	Converted urban renewal plans, tax delinquencies	5,458	1,184
Buffalo	Foreclosure procedure	100	10
Camden	City stock	Extensive	Not determined
Dayton	HUD	Uncertain*	4
Minneapolis	City stock	Uncertain*	300
Newark	Foreclosure procedure, gifts	Approximately 2,000	Not determined
Philadelphia	City stock, gifts, and HUD	20,000 to 35,000	74
Pittsburgh	City rentals and city stock	400	650
Rockford	HUD	Not specified	50
St. Louis	Foreclosure procedure	Several thousand	2,000
Washington	HUD	Uncertain*	All abandoned homes
Wilmington	City stock	2,000	78

*Regulated by number of HUD releases.
Source: Compiled by the authors.

TABLE 5.37

Comparison of Homestead Units

	Number of Units to Date	Additional Number Projected	Cost of Rehabilitation	Criteria for Unit and Neighborhood
Baltimore	105 in process	Not specified	$13,809 mean cost	"Cluster" in totally abandoned neighborhood; "scatter" in viable neighborhood with other development programs
Buffalo	1 in process	25 total	$6,000	Viable neighborhood; structural and financial feasibility
Camden	5	Not specified	Not specified	Not specified
Dayton	4 in program	150 during 1975	Not specified	Not specified
Minneapolis	9 in program	12 during 1975, 125 by 1980	$13,375 mean cost	Fair-market value of house must be higher than acquisition and rehabilitation costs.
Newark	About 300	Not specified	Not specified	Not specified
Philadelphia	31 completed and occupied	400 per year	$7,500 with sweat equity	Rehabilitable below fair-market value; moderate deterioration; vacancy less than 5%; property values $8,000 to $12,000
Pittsburgh	48	Not specified	$8,000 to $9,000	Unoccupied and tax delinquent or rented by city
Rockford	22	Not specified	$5,873 average	Structural and financial feasibility
St. Louis	300 in process	500 by 1979	Not specified	Below code, structurally sound
Washington	13 in process, 5 occupied	13 to 20 per year, depends on HUD	$17,500	HUD houses made available to city for homesteading
Wilmington	27 in program, 5 occupied	18 per year plus HUD houses acquired	$7,000	Vacancy less than 25%

Source: Compiled by the authors.

TABLE 5.38

Comparison of Homesteading Requirements

	Occupancy Requirements	Begin Rehabilitation	Code–Allowance Time
Baltimore	2 years from title acquisition	1 month	6 months (fire and safety) 2 years
Buffalo[a]	Not specified	Not specified	Not specified
Camden[b]	3 years	Not specified	Not specified
Dayton[b]	5 years	Not specified	Not specified
Minneapolis	3 years	1 month	All houses: 3 months (fire and safety codes) Using contractor: 6 months Without contractor: 1–1/2 years (HUD house), 2 years (all others)
Newark	5 years from title acquisition	Not specified	1 year
Philadelphia	5 years after occupancy begins	2 months after conveyance	4 months (fire and safety codes) 2 years
Pittsburgh[b]	2 years after occupancy begins	Not specified	Not specified
Rockford	4 years	60 days after conveyance	18 months
St. Louis	3 years from title acquisition	Varies by contractual agreement	2 years
Washington	5 years after occupancy begins	Counseling decision	3 months (fire and safety codes) 1 year
Wilmington	3 years after occupancy begins	Counseling decision	18 months

[a] No housing rehabilitation is in effect under homesteading ordinance.
[b] Other data on timing was not available.

Source: Compiled by the authors.

TABLE 5.39

Comparison of Support Services

	Special Financing	Support Programs
Baltimore	City loan—6% interest, 312 loan in historic area	Work write-up; counseling—financing, contractors, rehabilitation; community organizations; fence some abandoned properties
Buffalo	Rehabilitation Loan Fund—8% with 5-year city guarantee	Technical and contractor advice
Camden	None available	Bilingual specialist
Dayton	City loan—9 1/2% interest with 10% down payment	Financial counseling
Minneapolis	City, federal loans at 4%, 6%, 8% interest by income	MHRA aids owner in recovering investment in case of early sale; counseling—financing, contractor, procedure; neighborhood organizations; equal-opportunity employer
Newark	5-year city loan with balloon payment and refinancing with house as collateral	Financial counseling
Philadelphia	Local nonprofit loan—5 years; then state loan at 1% to 8% interest by income	Some rehabilitation done by city on all houses; some houses completely "rehabbed" by city; counseling—financing, contracting for rehabilitation; neighborhood organizations, extensive upgrading of city services; tax graduated for five years
Pittsburgh	Government loans available in 3 neighborhoods	Neighborhood organizations; city services upgraded
Rockford	Homestead board acquires loan, loans it to homesteader	Priority schedule written for homesteader; tool lending library; encourage cooperative purchases of materials; technical assistance; financial assistance
St. Louis	Lease-purchase agreement with down payment, monthly payments	Limited; no financial
Washington	Provision for conventional loans at 10% interest	Group meetings; extensive counseling—financing, homeownership; contracting for rehabilitation; neighborhood organizations
Wilmington	Conventional loans with city guarantee of 40% of loan	Technical assistance to encourage low and moderate income counseling—buddy system of homesteader/board member; priority work schedule, architect, volunteer labor

Source: Compiled by the authors.

106

TABLE 5.40

Comparison of Program Problems

City	Problems
Baltimore	Staff time to carry through program
Buffalo	Frame housing; two-year foreclosure procedure allows vandalism and deterioration
Camden	State law requires market-value sale to highest bidder, requires city loans to carry high interest rate
Dayton	Not reported
Minneapolis	None reported
Newark	State law requires market-value sale to highest bidder, requires city loans to carry high interest rate
Philadelphia	Large abandonment stock; additional Loan Fund staff*
Pittsburgh	Funds for rehabilitation
Rockford	None reported
St. Louis	Funds for rehabilitation; time to meet code inspections
Washington	Acquiring houses from HUD
Wilmington	Funds for acquisition; large abandoned stock; contractors meeting agreements.

* Provided in 1976 Budget.
Source: Compiled by the authors.

NOTES

1. U.S. Department of Housing and Urban Development, Office of Policy Development and Research, Neighborhood Preservation: A Catalog of Local Programs (Washington, D.C.: U.S. Government Printing Office, February 1975), p. 161.

2. Baltimore Department of Housing and Community Development, Homesteading (Baltimore, Md.: April 1975).

3. Baltimore Department of Housing and Community Development, The Settler (Baltimore, Md.: May 1975), p. 4.

4. Linda Joy Mandzak, "A Cost-Benefit Analysis of the Baltimore Urban Scattered-Site Homestead Program" (Baltimore, Md.: May 1975), p. 4.

5. Ibid., p. 8.

6. Interview with Roger Windsor, Director of HODP, in Baltimore, Maryland, 5 June 1975.

7. Mandzak, "A Cost-Benefit Analysis," p. 13.

8. Camden City Council, "Purposes of Homesteading," in Administrative Guidelines (Camden, N.J.: 1974), p. 1.

9. U.S. Bureau of Census, 1970.

10. Ibid.

11. Camden City Council, "Purpose of Homesteading," p. 1.

12. Camden City Council, "An Ordinance to Promote the Utilization of Existing Housing," Administrative Code, Ordinance MC-894, mimeographed (Camden, N. J.: 29 November 1974).

13. Minnesota Statute, Sections 462.415 to 462.711, 1974.

14. Minneapolis Housing and Redevelopment Authority, Minneapolis Urban Homesteading: Administrative Guidelines (Minneapolis, Minn.: 7 November 1974), cover.

15. Ibid., p. 1.

16. Minneapolis Housing and Redevelopment Authority, "Profile of Applicants in First Lottery" (Minneapolis, Minn.: 17 December 1974); "Applications for the Three Homes" (Minneapolis, Minn.: 28 April 1975).

17. Minneapolis Housing and Redevelopment Authority, Low Interest Loans and Grants, City of Minneapolis (Minneapolis, Minn.: 1974), p. 1.

18. Minneapolis Housing and Redevelopment Authority, Urban Homesteading Guidelines, p. 3.

19. Steven C. Rother, "Urban Homesteading: It May be One Way to Reclaim Abandoned City Dwellings," New Jersey Municipalities, January 1974, pp. 14-17.

20. U.S. Bureau of the Census, 1970.

21. Rother, "Urban Homesteading," p. 14.

22. California Senate, Committee on Government Organization, Urban Homesteading: Sweat Equity at Work Helping to Solve the Housing Problems, mimeographed (Sacramento, Calif.: 4 December 1974), pp. 25-26.

23. Rother, "Urban Homesteading," p. 17.

24. Joseph Miller, realtor, telephone conversation, 13 August 1975.

25. Philadelphia Urban Homestead Office, "Philadelphia Urban Homestead Program," unpublished report (Philadelphia, Pa.: 22 November 1974), p. 1.

26. The Philadelphia Partnership, "Urban Homesteading: A Status Report," unpublished report (Philadelphia, Pa.: November 1974), p. 3.

27. Ibid., p. 4.

28. "Ghetto Homesteaders," Time, 13 August 1973, p. 6.

29. Joseph Coleman, Esq., "Urban Homesteading: A Plan for Developing our New Frontiers" (paper presented to the Philadelphia Planning Commission, 1968), p. 4.

30. Philadelphia Urban Homestead Office, "Urban Homestead Program," p. 3; The Philadelphia Partnership, "Urban Homesteading," p. 4; Philadelphia City Codes,vol. 59 (Philadelphia), pp. 1-7; Philadelphia Urban Homestead Office, "The Facts about Urban Homesteading," pp. 1-5.

31. "Comments: Philadelphia's Urban Homesteading Ordinance: A Poor Beginning toward Reoccupying the Urban Ghost Town," Buffalo Law Review 23, no. 3 (Spring 1974): 735-63.

32. For the city of Pittsburgh's presentation to the state legislature on this issue, see Pennsylvania State Legislature, "Hearings on Pennsylvania House Bill 1703," mimeographed (1974), p. 1.

33. Ibid., p. 2.

34. Rockford Department of Community Renewal, "Urban Homesteading in Rockford," mimeographed (Rockford, Ill.: 1975), p. 4.

35. Ibid., p. 5.

36. Rockford Urban Homestead Board, "Urban Homestead Board Ordinance," mimeographed (Rockford, Ill.), p. 1.

37. Nick Tatro, "Urban Homesteaders Pay with Sweat," Norfolk Ledger-Star, 14 March 1975, p. 1.

38. Rockford City Council, "Urban Homestead Ordinance," February 25, 1974.

39. Rockford Department of Community Renewal, "Urban Homesteading in Rockford," mimeographed (Rockford, Ill.: 1975), p. 3.

40. Ibid., p. 6.

41. Ibid., p. 8.

42. U.S. Bureau of the Census, 1970.

43. "St. Louis Homestead Plan Now Entering Second Year," Journal of Housing (May 1974): 228.

44. Ibid.

45. Don Crinklaw, "What This City Needs is Some Good $1 Houses," St. Louisan, January 1974, p. 14.

46. Joseph J. Backers, The Land Reutilization Story (St. Louis, Mo.: Land Reutilization Authority, 2 January 1974), p. 1.

47. California Senate, Urban Homesteading: Sweat Equity, p. 23.

48. Backers, "Land Reutilization," p. 2.

49. Crinklaw, "What This City Needs," p. 14.

50. California Senate, Urban Homesteading: Sweat Equity, p. 24.

51. Crinklaw, "What This City Needs," p. 14.

52. Ibid.

53. "St. Louis Homestead Plan."

54. California Senate, Urban Homesteading: Sweat Equity,p. 22.

55. J. Moore, urban-homesteading counselor, personal interview, 31 May 1975.

56. Gail Bronson, "The Old Homestead," Wall Street Journal, 21 September 1973.

57. Wilmington City Council, "An Ordinance Amending the City Code by Adding a New Chapter 33A Entitled 'Homestead Program,'" Administrative Code (Wilmington, Del.: 17 May 1973).

58. Theodore Spaulding, Wilmington Homestead Director, personal interview, 4 June 1975.

59. Ibid.

60. Dee Wedemeyer, "Urban Homesteading," Nation's Cities, January 1975, p. 19.

61. Wilmington City Council, "Ordinance Amending Chapter 33A Homestead Program," Administrative Code (Wilmington, Del.: May 1973).

62. Wilmington City Council, "Ordinance to Grant a Partial Tax Exemption," Administrative Code (Wilmington, Del.: 21 August 1972).

63. U.S. Congress, House, Committee on the District of Columbia, Subcommittee on the Judiciary, Urban Homesteading: Hearings on H.R. 12197, 93rd Cong., 2nd sess., 1974, pp. 9-20.

64. The Wilmington Homestead Program, unpublished report (Wilmington, Del.: 1974), p. 1.

6

STATISTICAL ANALYSIS
OF HOMESTEADING ACCORDING
TO AFFECTED GROUPS

The in-depth case studies yielded detailed information on the individual operation of homesteading in 11 cities. Now it seemed appropriate to move from the specific descriptions toward a general policy theory. It was felt by the authors that information about the affected groups was essential in order to assess the impact of homesteading at this point. To our knowledge, no previous work had been done on opinions and reactions of the homesteaders, the homestead officials, or other citizens in the community. Problems and potential problems had been noted by some observers, but these had not been verified from the standpoint of the participants.

We were seeking to know what the composite homesteader was like, what the composite program was like, and what the composite effect was. Each affected group was separated and analyzed as a unit. The data from the questionnaire forms used in the case studies were then analyzed for this composite information.

Each of the three groups had a special relationship to homesteading. Each will be treated in a separate section in this chapter. The groups will not be compared because the questionnaire schedules differed according to each group's position vis-a-vis the program. It was felt that homesteaders, homestead officials, and civic leaders each perceived the problems and benefits of homesteading differently. Hypotheses were developed based on these separate group problems. These hypotheses will be stated and tested in the three sections that follow.

CIVIC LEADERS

Questionnaire forms were sent to 22 civic leaders, two in each homestead city. We requested an officer of the chamber of commerce to complete one questionnaire and any member of the board of realtors to complete the other. Because homesteading was a small pilot program in many cities and rather new, its impact on the marketplace and the community at large could not be felt by most citizens. However, we believed that any slight change would be noticed by realtors and/or chamber-of-commerce leaders. There were 14 forms completed and returned.

The questionnaires were designed to gather data that would address the following problems: Does the community at large support the concept of homesteading? Does the community feel that homesteading will improve the city? If so, how? Has business been affected by homesteading? If so, how has it been affected? These questions were hypothesized as follows:

Hypothesis I: If urban homesteading exists in a city, community
                leaders will respond to its presence.
Hypothesis II: If urban homesteading exists in a city, community
                leaders perceive improvements in the city.
Hypothesis III: If urban homesteading exists in a city, community
                leaders will observe a change in business activities.

Hypothesis I

If urban homesteading exists in a city, community leaders will respond to its presence.

Community support is essential to the success of any policy. For many cities homesteading represented an initial venture into housing policy. There was the possibility present for opposition to city intervention in this way; homesteading as implemented allowed certain citizens to derive unusual benefits that might cause resentments from other citizens. The civic leaders chosen were expected to have sensitivity to broad citizen response to public housing policy.

Operational Terms

Community-leaders' responses were operationalized by three questions: 1. Do you believe homesteading will prevent further neighborhood abandonment and deterioration? 2. Are you aware of any citizen opposition to the program? 3. Would you recommend homesteading to other cities that may be considering the program?

Findings

    In answer to the first question, 9 of the 14 civic leaders said yes.
They believed that urban homesteading would prevent further neighborhood abandonment and deterioration. This positive community
support is probably due to the trend toward rehabilitation and conservation that has become apparent recently. Another factor which
may have influenced this response is the widespread disenchantment
in many cities with demolition policies. Although demolition has
resulted in some cosmetic improvements to cities, neighborhoods
have continued to deteriorate at an increasing rate.

    Responding to the second question concerning citizen opposition
to homesteading, none of the civic leaders noted any citizen opposition to homesteading. This total endorsement as perceived by the
leaders may be due to their awareness of rising citizen resentments
to present housing policy. Displacement and relocation along with
the increased cost of housing have fueled these resentments. Relocation provoked widespread citizen protests from both middle- and
lower-income groups. The decrease in the housing supply meant
that the demand could only be met with increased prices. Relocatees
needed to spend a larger proportion of their incomes for housing.
This economic and psychological disruption led to organized citizen
protest in some cities. The fact that community leaders perceived no
opposition to the program may also have been due to the current
economic situation. Inflation, high cost of building, high interest
rates, and a tight money market have combined to create an atmos-
phere conducive to rehabilitation rather than new construction.

    The fact that 12 of the 14 civic leaders answered the third ques-
tion by stating that they would recommend homesteading to other
cities indicates that they believe homesteading will have positive
results in their own city and will be beneficial to others.

Conclusions

    The high percentage of positive responses to all three questions
tends to support hypothesis I. Based on the opinions of chamber of
commerce leaders and board of realty members, civic leaders give
overwhelming support to homesteading, and they also indicated that
the community climate is favorable. The favorable community climate may be due to the fact that in each homestead city abandoned
structures and deteriorated neighborhoods are present in great
numbers. Civic leaders perceived these problems as critical. These
environmental factors would tend to create a positive attitude to any
alternatives to past policies. Further, homesteading has a very

romantic appeal to citizens. This appeal activates latent needs of citizens to serve their communities by a pioneering spirit, by helping to restore inner cities, and by fostering a sense of control over one's destiny.

It appears that homesteading operates in a hospitable environment. Does it help to improve that environment?

TABLE 6.1

Distribution of Benefits to the City
as Seen by Civic Leaders*

Benefit	Number	Percent
Financial		
Improve tax base	4	36
Use of abandoned houses	2	18
Combination	5	46
Total	11	
Social		
Neighborhood stability	2	17
Citizen opportunity	1	8
Combination	9	75
Total	12	
Cosmetic		
Improved appearance	5	45
Discourages vandalism	0	
Combination	6	55
Total	11	

*Most of the civic leaders perceived more than one category of benefits.

Note: Positive benefits to the city were claimed by 12 of 14 respondents. One claimed no benefits. One replied, "don't know."

Source: Compiled by the authors.

Hypothesis II

If urban homesteading exists in a city, then community leaders perceive improvements in the city.

A decent home and suitable environment were adopted as primary housing goals in the federal Housing Act of 1949.[1] The political and economic goals of our government are to maximize the well-being of all citizens. Society interprets this to mean the social as well as the economic well-being. The Housing Act of 1949 stated this goal as it related to housing needs. A primary consideration for any public policy is that it benefit the city. Improvements to the city could be such benefits.

Operational Terms

Improvements in the city is operationalized as "benefits to the city." "Benefits to the city" is further operationalized as financial benefits, social benefits, and cosmetic benefits. Those who believed homesteading benefits the city were asked a probing question. This group of respondents is referred to as the "positive-benefits" group. The probing question delineated the benefits into three categories: financial, social, cosmetic.

Findings

The responses to the questions about benefits were very positive, as can be seen in Table 6.1. The few negative responses were related by the respondents to the small size of the program and/or to its recent adoption. Of the 14 respondents, 12 claimed that homesteading benefits the city. The responses were evenly distributed among the three categories. Of the 12 "positive benefit" responses, 11 mentioned financial benefits; 6 of these stated that the financial benefits were evident in an increased tax base or in increased use of abandoned housing. The other five respondents indicated both benefits were present. A possible explanation of the strong value given financial benefits may be that civic leaders are aware of the high cost of maintaining abandoned properties and recognize that using these properties for urban homesteading is less costly. Obviously, occupying abandoned houses will lead to an increased tax base, eventually, and is a measurable financial benefit to the city.

Of the positive-benefit group, 12 cited social benefits for either citizens or neighborhoods or both. Social benefits are expressions of "suitable environment" which comes from the theory of neighborhood preservation. Social benefits can be measured against the social costs of the conditions that existed in neighborhoods prior to homesteading. The fact that civic leaders recognize the social benefits implies that they also recognize the social costs of abandonment and neighborhood deterioration. Possibly they observed positive changes occurring in neighborhood life in homestead areas; that is, increased activity in neighborhood organization and citizen participation.

Of the positive-benefits group, 11 noted cosmetic changes that improved the appearance of the city. Both "improved appearance" and "lessened vandalism" were mentioned by six respondents. Cosmetic benefits would be noticed by civic leaders because of their interest in the city's appearance. A change toward better maintenance of an area could have been noted from observation of additional renovation, cleaner yards, and less vandalism.

Conclusions

On the basis of the total response to the questions on benefits to the city, nearly all the respondents believed homesteading benefits the city and cited all three types of benefits. These relationships tend to support hypothesis II. Whether the benefits were measurable in dollars (financially) or in human needs met (socially) or in appearance of an area (cosmetically), they were all present in nearly equal proportions. The perceptions of civic leaders could have been based on observation as well as city reports and media presentations.

Hypothesis III

If urban homesteading exists in a city, civic leaders observe a change in business activity.

If the theory of neighborhood preservation is viable in homesteading areas, then small neighborhood businesses should improve or should return to the area if they have left. Larger businesses in neighborhood centers should also benefit from homesteading. According to Jane Jacobs, neighborhood vitality is measured in terms of multiple uses of land.[2] Small and large businesses should be present in vital neighborhoods. Improved business would be a second-order impact of homesteading that would result indirectly from the rehabilitation of houses and the resulting neighborhood changes.

Operational Terms

Business in the community was operationalized by three questions: 1. Has homesteading affected your business in any way? 2. Do you believe other businesses in the community have been affected by homesteading? 3. If so, what businesses specifically?

Findings

In response to the first question, eight of the civic leaders have experienced no change in their businesses. Only four civic leaders knew of other businesses that had been affected. Three were contracting firms and one was a real-estate company. The small number of responses can be attributed to the fact that it is too soon to measure the impact on business in any of the homestead cities. Even the first-order impacts cannot be measured accurately until the homesteaders have gained clear title. Most homesteaders are probably too involved with the problems of rehabilitation and too deeply in debt to consider other types of purchases. It was to be expected, then, that three of the known businesses that were affected were contracting firms. It is very interesting to note that a real-estate business was cited as the other business affected. This may mean that homesteading is stimulating interest in other homes in the neighborhood that may be for sale. It seems likely that businesses, other than housing-related ones, will not show a change due to homesteading for at least three years. Perhaps if more emphasis is placed on homesteading commercial property, the impact may be felt sooner.

Conclusions

There seems to be a small relationship between homesteading and certain types of businesses, mainly those directly related to housing rehabilitation. Effects on other businesses in the community have not been observed by civic leaders. This may be due to the fact that homesteading has not been in existence long enough to attract businesses back into neighborhoods where they may have formerly existed; or it may be that homesteaders have not been relocated long enough to exert an impact on existing business.

HOMESTEAD OFFICIALS

A questionnaire schedule was sent to an official of the homestead program in every city. It was felt that officials could provide more detailed information on goals than could be gleaned from a legal document. Often short-term goals, known mostly by officials, can give insights that help explain certain procedures or practices. The implementation schedule and program are areas that a program official has usually developed himself. Knowledge of the areas of emphasis from the official's viewpoint was therefore considered important. Problems and opinions of officials, though necessarily biased to the program, might provide guidelines as well as justifications. Questionnaire forms were mailed to 12 officials. Eight completed and returned the form. This represented 66.7 percent of the total sample.

The questions of special interest had to do with program administration, problems, and future development possibilities. Specifically,

we sought information from the officials in the following areas:
1. Does the type of administration affect the homesteading program?
2. What problems do officials encounter, and how do those problems
affect the program? 3. Are there possible uses of a homestead policy
other than rehabilitation of abandoned single-family dwellings?

The hypotheses formulated were as follows:

Hypothesis I: If there is a difference in administrative structure in
                cities with similar numbers of available houses, the
                programs will differ.

Hypothesis II: If there is a difference in the size of the urban-home-
                stead program, then the problems encountered will
                differ.

Hypothesis III: In the opinion of urban-homestead officials, there are
                possible adaptations of the single-family-dwelling
                program.

Hypothesis I

If there is a difference in administrative structure, in cities with
similar numbers of available houses, the programs will differ.

Differences in administrative structure have already been described in the case-studies analyses. We hypothesized that these
differences would affect the program. It seemed logical that this
might happen because type and size of management has always been
considered directly related to type and size of business activity. We
discovered in our city analysis that there were two main types of
administrative structures in homestead cities: a separate homestead
agency, operating as an autonomous department of the city and a
homestead agency operating within another department of the city.

On the one hand, one could assume that a separate homestead
agency would be able to handle a larger program because the staff
would not have other programs to drain off its time and energy. On
the other hand, one could assume that a homesteading office within
another agency might be able to handle a larger program because it
would have more resources available to it—more staff and more
skills. In order to try to find out how these administrative structures
differed, the size of the housing stock would have to be controlled so
that only the administration was being measured. We needed to com-
pare only cities with a relatively similar number of available houses.
If we compared cities with unequal-sized housing stock, we might
not have known whether the administration or the available houses had
affected the size of the program.

Operational Terms

Administrative agency is operationalized by the type of administration specified by the official, that is, either a separate agency or one
that is part of another city agency. Differing programs were operationalized as the number of houses in the program. The control is
operationalized as the number of houses available for homesteading.

TABLE 6.2

Number of Homesteads According to Type of Agency*

Number of Homesteads	Homestead Administration	
	Independent Agency	Within Another Agency
1 - 10	2	1
11 - 50	2	1
51 - 300	—	1

*Control not used; see "Findings."
Source: Compiled by the authors.

Findings

With the control, there was an almost equal division of agencies
between separate administration and administration within another
agency. Without the control, the findings were similar. Therefore,
we omitted the tabulation that included the control. It seemed unneces-
sary. The reason for these findings might be that in practice the
separate homestead agency must rely on other agencies within the
city as much as if it were a part of another agency. Licenses and
inspections, tax assessors, code enforcement, and possibly other
agencies all play a part in the administration of a homestead program.
The same resources would have to be available to the independent
homestead agency as to the one that is within another agency. In
practice it seems it would be impossible for the separate agency to
remain independent of other departments and devote its full time to
homesteading. Interdepartmental bureaucratic problems would exist
under both types of program.

Conclusions

The hypothesis is not supported by the data. We find little relationship between the type of administrative structure and the size of

the programs. Both types of administration were present in programs of all sizes. Regardless of the number of houses in the program or the number of houses available for homesteading, the administrative agency follows either pattern. Before our on-site inspections, we would have thought that an agency that was part of another group would have lost its goals or its direction and would have been generally affected by the parent agency. Our on-site inspection of Baltimore dissuaded us from this belief. This analysis confirms our observations.

Hypothesis II

If there is a difference in the size of the urban-homestead program, then the problems encountered will be different.

In reviewing the literature, we noted many authors who predicted that homesteading would never become a large enough program to make a dent in the problem of abandoned housing or neighborhood deterioration. Their thinking was based on the legal and financial problems that homesteading engendered both for the city and the homesteader. We wanted to test this observation empirically in order to find out if the problems of homesteading affected the size of the program. If the critics of homesteading were correct, cities with many financial and legal problems would have smaller homesteading programs than the cities with fewer such problems.

Operational Terms

The problems encountered were defined in the response to an open-ended question posed to homestead officials: What are the major

TABLE 6.3

Problems Encountered According to Number of Homesteads
as Reported by Homestead Officials

Problems	Number of Homesteads		
	1–10	11–50	51–300
Financing	0	1	1
Time	1	1	1
None	1	—	—

Note: n = 7; no response = 1.
Source: Compiled by the authors.

problems with the program? The answers fell into five values. These
were divided into two major categories of problems: the financing
of the rehabilitation and the time period required from acquisition
to occupancy. The size of the program refers to the number of houses
in the program. This was operationalized into three groups based on
the clustering that occurred in the officials' answers. The three
program sizes are those with 1 to 10 homesteads, those with 11 to 50
homesteads, and those with 51 to 300 homesteads.

Findings

Table 6.3 shows that time is a problem related to programs of
all sizes. Financing problems seem to beset the medium- and large-
sized programs. It may be significant that the only program with no
perceived problems was in the smallest category.

The most evident problems to officials were time and financing.
Officials were probably viewing these problems from the standpoint
of expediting the homestead program and also from the standpoint of
the homesteaders—their needs and their frustrations. Financing is
complicated for both. The homestead program needs funds to acquire
stock and also to provide guarantees for loans and/or the loan funds
themselves. Homesteaders need low-interest loans. In many instances
they are paying rent while rehabilitating their homes. Homestead
neighborhoods are often redlined by conventional lending institutions.
There are no federal funds available for homestead loans. City
bonding limits frequently prohibit the cities from floating bonds for
homesteading. These are just some of the many financing problems
that could beset a homestead program.

The time problem has multiple ramifications also. The homestead
official sees time as a problem for several reasons. If abandoned
houses are not obtained quickly, they may deteriorate beyond reclamation and further the deterioration process in their neighborhoods.
Additionally, the sooner the houses are brought into the program,
the sooner they can be restored to the tax roles and justify the program budgetwise. Time is a major factor to the homesteader because
he needs to occupy his house quickly in order to curtail his living
expenses in another dwelling. The time when the homestead is unoccupied is frequently when the property is vandalized. The sooner
the homesteader occupies his homestead and begins to fulfill the
living requirements, the sooner he will obtain equity. Time problems
are complicated by delays in procuring funding, delays on the part
of contractors, and delays in the legal clarification of ownership and
clear title. Almost all of the program problems that the officials
cited are related to either finance or time problems.

Conclusions

The hypothesis appears to be supported by the data. The problems encountered differ with different-sized programs. However, the data does not necessarily support the theorists who believed the problems would tend to keep the program small. Perhaps the directors of the small programs did not choose to identify their problems; or perhaps these problems are common to all housing (homeownership) programs and did not seem notable to the directors. Of the directors reporting, it appears plain that problems of time are present in all-sized programs. Financing as a problem tends to appear in medium- and large-sized programs.

Hypothesis III

In the opinion of urban homestead officials, there are possible adaptations of the single-family-dwelling program.

We were particularly interested in officials' opinions regarding homesteading in areas other than single-family dwellings. The possibility of using vacant land might be important to the cities that may have already done much clearance and demolition and not been successful in redeveloping that land. The possibility of homesteading abandoned commercial property seemed to present a possible method of restoring multiple uses and services to deteriorating neighborhoods. Abandoned multiple-family units, large apartments, and tenements are serious problems in some of the very large cities of our nation. Could these be adapted for homesteading? James Davis stressed the vacant-land-homesteading theory in his proposal in 1970.[3] Louis Stone was an early proponent of condominium ownership of public-housing units.[4] His homestead proposal for this use was reported in 1972. Restoring multiple uses for neighborhood revitalization is a major aspect of Jane Jacobs' theory of diversity.[5] Would the values of homeownership be as positive within these varied frameworks? The opinions of homestead officials were sought in order to assess some of the future possibilities for homesteading.

Operational Terms

The adaptations that officials were requested to assess were vacant land homesteading, multi-family-unit homesteading, and commercial-property homesteading. These were the operational terms for homesteading adaptations.

TABLE 6.4

Possible Homesteading Adaptations According to Officials

Opinion of Officials	Commercial	Multi-family	Vacant Land
Yes			
Number	3	2	5
Percent	38*	25	63
Maybe			
Number	3	3	0
Percent	38	38	0
No			
Number	2	3	1
Percent	25	38	13
No Response			
Number	0	0	2
Percent	0	0	25
Total			
Number	8	8	8
Percent	100	100	100

*Percentages rounded off.
Note : n = 8.
Source: Compiled by the authors.

Findings

The officials recognized the possiblity of all three types of adaptations. The large percentage who responded "yes" to vacant-land adaptation probably reflects the fact that many cities have included this option in their ordinances but have not yet implemented it to any extent. Buffalo is preparing for this type of homesteading at present. This appeared to be a certain option, since no officials even said "maybe." It seems logical to combine the "yes" and "maybe" responses as one positive response because many of the "yes" responses may indicate that the adaptation is already being implemented and the "maybe" responses may mean the adaptation is under consideration.

When the top two response categories are combined, there is strong support for all three adaptations: 76 percent favor commercial homesteading; 63 percent favor multi-family homesteading; 63 percent favor vacant-land homesteading. We have already noted that some of the cities have plans to implement these adaptations. At least two cities have provisions for nonprofit corporations to become home-steaders (Minneapolis and Philadelphia). These corporations must undertake supervision and servicing for the occupancy period. The multi-family units that they homestead must benefit low-income people. This represents another possible variation for homesteading.

Conclusion

Historically, homesteading has been linked to the concept of "freeholders," which implies single families. Some officials may cling to this concept, and that may explain why they could not recog-nize any other possibilities. The average homestead stock does not contain multi-family dwellings. Officials in such cities would not see the need for this adaptation. None of the ordinances reviewed contained provisions for condominium ownership. Therefore this possibility may have been overlooked by the officials who responded negatively. If a homestead neighborhood had no commercial property, the official would not have recognized this possibility. In addition, some cities have legal restraints forbidding city gifts to business enterprises This would explain the negative response to commercial adaptations.

It is apparent that there is high agreement among homestead officials that possible adaptations of homesteading other than single-family units are desirable. The hypothesis is supported by the data. It appears that homesteading has the possibility for growth and variation in many United States cities.

HOMESTEADERS

For the purposes of this study, homesteader was defined as the program participant who had occupied his or her homestead under the aegis of the local urban-homesteading program for a period of time. It did not include those who had not yet moved into their home-steads. This limitation was made to help ensure adequate acquain-tance with the neighborhood, the house, and the program by the re-spondents. Out of 241 homestead questionnaire forms, 60 were com-pleted and returned. These 60 represent the first attempt to get opinions from homesteaders. Previous profiles have been limited to socioeconomic data. In a few of the homestead cities such profiles have been used for annual reports by the city departments. The data presented here represents homesteaders' profiles and opinions from ten cities. It is a unique report in this respect.

Urban housing needs, as discussed in Chapter 2, are greatest among the low income. Urban housing cycles often result in abandonment of sound structures within certain neighborhoods. This abandonment occurs in lower-income neighborhoods, affecting the low-income housing supply. Low-income persons are the least able to maintain property financially. The abandonment often spreads to adjacent neighborhoods, which may be moderate- to middle-income housing. The spread of abandonment, or blight, affects the neighborhood stability. It seems to be more pervasive in neighborhoods with a low percentage of homeownership. Once a neighborhood begins to be affected, strong efforts by local residents are necessary to reverse the process. In cases cited in Chapter 2, the promotion of economic and racial integration stabilized the neighborhood.

With this theoretical background, it seemed important to study the homesteaders as a first-order impact of homesteading. In some cities urban homesteading is assumed to promote neighborhood stability. Therefore the following problems were addressed in this study:

1. What socioeconomic groups benefit directly from urban homesteading?
2. Does homesteading make homeownership available to people who could not otherwise own homes?
3. Does income level of homesteaders affect the type of problems encountered in homesteading?
4. Are homesteaders discouraged by the program-related problems?
5. Does homesteading improve the vitality of neighborhoods?

These problems were formed into the following hypotheses:

Hypothesis I: Homesteaders represent a homogeneous socio-economic group.

Hypothesis II: If urban homesteading exists, certain citizens have the opportunity for homeownership.

Hypothesis III:If homesteaders are in certain income groups, this will be reflected in their racial characteristics and the problems they encounter.
    A. Problems encountered by homesteaders are related to their income.
    B. There is a relationship between the income of the homesteaders and the type of financing used.
    C. Higher income whites are more likely to homestead than higher income blacks.

Hypothesis IV:If certain homesteading problems and finance methods exist, then homesteader satisfaction is affected.

TABLE 6.5

Socioeconomic Description of Homesteaders

Description	Adjusted Percentages*
Age	
Under 30	37
31 to 40	24
41 to 50	12
51 and over	27
No response	—
Occupation	
Professional–technical	47
Managers	5
Service workers	38
Other	10
Race	
Black	56
White	44
No response	—
Education	
Under twelfth grade	24
High-school graduate	24
College incomplete	17
College graduate	19
Graduate work	17
No response	—
Income	
0 to $9,000	41
$10,000 to $19,000	41
$20,000 to $29,000	10
$30,000 and over	7
No response	—

*Percentages are rounded off. The adjusted percentages are based on the total number responding in each category.

Note: n = 60.

Source: Compiled by the authors.

A. Satisfaction is affected by problems of the homesteaders.
B. Satisfaction with the program is affected by the
   finance method used by homesteaders
Hypothesis V: Homesteaders perceive greater stability in homestead neighborhoods than in former neighborhoods.

Hypothesis I

Homesteaders represent a homogeneous socio-economic group.
Homesteading generally evokes interest about the primary benefit
group. People want to know who receives the houses, what type of
person the homesteader is, and what his or her housing needs are.
This information, socioeconomic data, is often included in annual
reports from the urban-homestead office. It represents a first-order
impact of the program policy. Most homeownership policies have primarily benefited specific socioeconomic groups, such as Federal
Home Agency loans to middle- and upper-income persons. One might
assume that this program is likewise directed to a particular group.

Operational Terms

Socioeconomic group is operationalized as age, race, occupation,
education, and income. Occupation included categories of professional-
technical, service workers, managers, and others. The technical
included some skilled and semiskilled occupations. Service workers
included salespeople as well. Income is divided into four integral
categories. Homogeneous is defined as within a single category of
the socioeconomic values.

Findings

The homesteaders are well distributed within the population
according to the statistics gathered. An analysis of age reveals a
fairly even distribution in four age categories, with the least number
of homesteaders in the 41 to 50 age group. Distribution by race
reveals an almost equal division between blacks and whites. Although
there were a few other occupations represented, the homesteaders
were mainly grouped in professional-technical and service-worker
categories. The homesteaders were almost evenly divided between
the four education groups, with the largest percentage in the first
category, up to twelfth grade (24%), and the second category, high-
school graduate (24%).

Income specified here is the take-home pay for the entire household, not for one wage earner. Many of the homesteaders reported
that other wage earners lived in the same household. Income of
homesteaders in Table 6.5 was dispersed: It spread from unemployed
to beyond $30,000. Most of the homesteaders represented the 0-to-
$9,000 and $10,000-to-$19,000 income groups. The mode (17 re-
spondents) is the same in each of those two groups.

Conclusions

The hypothesis is not supported by the data. In none of the operationalized characteristics were significant differences present that
would suggest a homogeneity among the homesteader group. This
surprising finding might reflect a trend toward inner-city living. A
program designed to encourage city living might appeal to many who
want to move into the city or stay within the city. Possibly this motivation was combined with a desire to participate in the urban problem-
solving programs. Such idealists would choose to invest in a blighted
neighborhood with the expectation of rebuilding the area. These
speculations could explain the presence of those socioeconomic groups
who have a wide choice of housing locations.

The trend toward conservation of all resources might operate in
homesteading, also. All groups of people are being affected by the
need and demand for conservation. This is perhaps especially well
recognized by the upper-educated group. Conservation or recycling
of housing would seem a logical solution to the housing shortage and
high construction prices. Similarly, this moderately priced housing
with homeowner-equity possibilities would promote the upward social
mobility of lower- and moderate-income people. The young homesteaders might possibly be attracted for idealistic reasons. They may
have rising incomes, a pioneer spirit, or an urban social consciousness

The homesteaders are 56 percent black. When this is compared to
the United States, 11% of the population is black.[6] The recent shifts
of this population to urban centers has resulted in the inner-city areas
becoming nearly all black. Therefore, the 56 percent black among
homesteaders is closer to the reality of inner-city neighborhoods
where homestead sites may be located.

The income of the homesteaders was recorded by only 41 respondents. This could be due to uncertain circumstances (several
said that they did not know what their pay would be) or the desire to
maintain privacy in this area. Some may not have understood the
question (What do you estimate the take-home pay for this entire
household to be in 1975?). This was the area of weakest response by
the homesteaders.

Hypothesis II

If urban homesteading exists, certain citizens have the opportunity for homeownership.

Since providing homeownership is a key point in this policy, it
seemed appropriate to discover whether this opportunity was being
offered to people who did not and/or could not own homes. Homeownership has been identified in Chapter 2 as a criterion of neighborhood stability. In addition, the accumulation of equity through
homeownership is considered an incentive for owning one's home
and a mechanism for upward social mobility. For most people, a
home is their major investment. Most of their assets are in the
property.

Operational Terms

Certain citizens are operationalized as homesteaders who would
not or could not own their own home without homesteading. Home

TABLE 6.6

Opportunity for Homeownership

Homesteader Responses	Homeownership		
	First Home to Own	Without Home- steading	Is Main Benefit of Homesteading
Yes			
Percent	62	40	65
Number	37	24	39
No			
Percent	38	50	7
Number	23	30	4
Don't know			
Percent	n.a.*	10	28
Number	n.a.	6	17
Total			
Percent	100	100	100
Number	60	60	60

*Not applicable.
Note: n = 60.
Source: Compiled by the authors.

ownership is operationalized by three questions: 1. Is this your first
home to own? 2. Without homesteading would you have attempted
to buy a home? 3. What benefits have you gained from homesteading?
If homeownership was the main benefit answered, this became the
basis of the data for this question.

Findings

The majority (62 percent) of respondents said that this was their
first home to own. There is a difference in younger and older homesteaders who own a home for the first time. The younger may have
realistic ambitions of eventual homeownership as their income rises;
the older may have no other opportunity to own a home. There were
50 percent of the respondents who said they would not have attempted
to buy a home without homesteading. This is more conclusive; the
younger might be able to become homeowners sooner with homesteading but not exclusively with homesteading. Homeownership was
listed by 65 percent of the respondents as the main benefit from homesteading. To many, the main benefit was described as "pride in
homeownership," "personal satisfaction in homeownership" and
"lower living costs." These are all interpreted here to mean that
homeownership was their main benefit.

Conclusion

The data tend to support the hypothesis. They indicate that homesteading is reaching a group of citizens who could not otherwise avail
themselves of ownership. The group who said this was not their first
home to own chose to live in the inner city. Reasons for this choice
could be idealism of social justice for residents of the inner city,
transportation advantages in the city, lower living costs, or accessi-
bility to city's cultural life. The other benefits of homesteading were
of more value to them than homeownership, possibly.

The negative response to the question about attempting to buy a
home without homesteading supports the hypothesis. The 10 percent
of "don't know's" may be young persons not yet able to assess their
homeownership possibilities on the open market. The fact that only
7 percent did not cite homeownership as the main benefit of homesteading is notable. The group who responded "don't know" to main
benefit include many who felt the program was too young to determine
the benefits.

Hypothesis III

If homesteaders are in certain income groups, this will be reflected in their racial characteristics and the problems they encounter.

According to urban-housing theory, the lower-income group does not have the means to provide adequate property maintenance. The costs of maintenance of standard housing are greater than the amount the poor can allocate from their income. This situation is exacerbated by, as well as partially responsible for, the practice of redlining. Loan institutions, knowing the probabilities of little or no maintenance of property in some neighborhoods, refuse to allow investments in these areas. Limited access to the capital market discourages those willing and able to invest in maintaining their property within these neighborhoods. This "prisoner's dilemma" is coupled with the practice of discrimination against racial minorities. They find it difficult if not impossible to maintain their property through their own resources or to acquire the necessary financing. This situation would seem to exist to a lesser degree among moderate-income persons also.

Subhypothesis A. Problems encountered by homesteaders are related to their income.

TABLE 6.7

Homesteader Problems According to Income

Problems	Up to $10,000	$10,000 to $19,000	$20,000 to $29,000	$30,000 and over	Total*
Personal					
Finance	4	6	0	1	11
Labor, parts, and time	1	4	2	0	7
Program					
Process	1	5	2	0	8
Legal	3	2	0	2	7
Neighborhood					
Security	0	1	1	0	2
Cooperation	2	2	0	0	4

*Multiple responses were given.
Note: n = 39 responses out of a possible 180.
Source: Compiled by the authors.

Operational Terms

Problems that homesteaders cited on the questionnaire forms
were divided into three areas: personal problems, program problems, and neighborhood problems. Income is operationalized into
four integral categories. Income is the independent variable in
all three of these subhypotheses and will be defined the same for
each. It refers to the take-home pay of the entire household.

Findings

There were only 39 responses out of a possible 180 problems.
Multiple responses were possible for the 60 respondents. It is
notable that 20 (51 percent of the 39 responses) were in the $10,000
to $19,000 category. Of the total responses, 46 percent of the prob-
lems cited were personal. Among personal problems, 61 percent
of the responses dealt with financing. This is the largest percentage
of responses. Program problems comprised 38 percent of the responses. Only six responses indicated that neighborhood problems
were present.

Conclusions

Clearly, personal finance was the main problem area. The
$10,000-to-$19,000 group seemed to perceive more problems than
any other. This may have been due to age or to rising expectations.
We conjecture that this category includes many young, upwardly
mobile persons. They would have less experience in finance and
therefore encounter more problems in that area.

In the group with incomes under $10,000, personal finance was
also mentioned most frequently. This is an expected finding, according to the theory of urban housing. This category of up to
$10,000, however, comprises 28 percent of the total number of
responses. The $10,000-to-$19,000 group comprises 51 percent
of the total number of responses. However, each group represents
only 17 (41 percent) of the total number of respondents (Table 45).
The upper-income group perceives the same problems as the other
groups. There seems to be little relationship between type of problem and income. No problem is present in only one income category. The amount of problems reported is not directional, as we
would have assumed from the theory. The lowest income category
of up to $10,000 does not have the highest percentage of problems,
even when compared to the percentage they represent of the total
group of respondents.

Finance problems, which are the main complaints, are dispersed among all income categories. These could be of several types. They might be an expression of the impatience with the procedures and the red tape necessary to obtain financing; they might be problems of frustration due to inability to get loan money or due to legal complications or lending policies. The wide variety of finance problems could easily explain why all income groups had complaints of this nature.

Neighborhood problems appear to be the least significant. No one in the highest income category indicated neighborhood problems. Perhaps persons willing to homestead have a lower perception of what constitutes a neighborhood problem than other persons: Some adjustments are always necessary in any new situation.

Since there is no significant relationship, subhypothesis A is not supported.

Subhypothesis B. There is a relationship between the income of the homesteaders and the type of financing used.

Operational Terms

The type of financing refers to the loan procedure. There were four types of loans mentioned: conventional loans, city-sponsored or specified government loans (hereafter referred to as government loans), personal savings, and combinations of outside loans with personal savings. Those respondents with combinations were placed in the category of the outside loan specified, that is, conventional

TABLE 6.8

Loan Source According to Income

| Loan Source | Income Categories* | | | |
	0 to $9,000	$10,000 to $19,000	$20,000 and over	Total
Personal savings	5	4	2	11
Conventional loan	6	2	1	9
Government loan	5	11	4	20
Total	16	17	7	40

*Many respondents did not supply income information.
Note: n = 40.
Source: Compiled by the authors.

loans or government loans. The government loans, as described in
Chapter 5, are available in some of the cities. These are preferable
for most people because they are easier to get, bear lower interest
rates, and either have longer terms or can be refinanced. Special-
funding sources with similar features that are available only to
homesteaders (such as Philadelphia's Urban Homestead Finance
Corporation, Pittsburgh's Scaife Foundation for certain neighborhoods, and Wilmington City Housing Corporation) are included as
government loans.

Findings

Respondents in the lowest income category are evenly dispersed
among the loan sources. The other two categories are more heavily
represented in the government loan value. Conventional loans, generally readily available to upper-income categories, are used the
least. Of the 11 homesteaders using personal savings, 5 were in the
lowest income group.

Conclusions

We assume that most homesteaders would use the low-interest
government loan if it were available. Where it is not available, urban-

TABLE 6.9

Income According to Race among Homesteaders

Race	Income		Total
	Lower (0 to $9,000)	Higher ($10,000 and over)	
Black			
Number	12	10	22
Percent	71	42	
White			
Number	5	14	19
Percent	29	58	
Total			
Number	17	24	41
Percent	100	100	

Note: n = 41.
Source: Compiled by the authors.

housing theory would lead us to assume that fewer persons would be homesteaders as income decreases. Yet, we found that the majority of the homesteaders using personal savings or having conventional loans are in the 0-to-$9,000 category. Personal savings might be used by those unable to procure conventional loans. The attraction of homesteading apparently is great enough that lower-income persons participate even though no financial services are offered. Programs without loans do have low-to-moderate (0-to-$9,000)-income home-steaders. Since there is no significant relationship, subhypothesis B is not supported.

Subhypothesis C. Higher-income whites are more likely to home-stead than higher-income blacks.

Operational Terms

Higher income is operationalized to mean income of $10,000 and over. Race is defined as black and white.

Findings

There were 41 homesteaders who responded to both questions regarding race and income. The blacks were slightly more repre-sented in the lower-income category (12 out of 22). The whites were overwhelmingly in the higher-income category (14 out of 19). The racial groups within each income category are similarly spread. Among the lower-income group, 71% were black. Among the higher-income group, 58% were white.

Conclusions

The data tends to support subhypothesis C. Although the blacks are numerous in the higher-income group, most (58%) are white. This would be expected, since there are more white higher-income persons in the United States than black. Any policy that appeals to higher-income will have more white participation than black among that income level. We assume from the theory establishing home-steading that the neighborhood probably tended toward low-moderate income and toward black. The higher-income blacks may be reluc-tant to settle in an area of low-income blacks. Possibly they have struggled to avoid living as the poor live. Possibly, too, they would not want to be mistaken for poor residents. Higher-income whites would not be mistaken for low-income, nonmobile blacks. This finding of higher-income whites as homesteaders suggests that eco-nomic and racial integration seem to be occurring in homestead neighborhoods.

Since the only subhypothesis that was supported was C, concerning race, hypothesis III is not proven. Only race tends to be related to income among homesteaders. Problems encountered and the type of loan used do not seem related to income. One reason for these results would be that only two-thirds of the returns gave income information. This missing data could be significant. In education, about half (28 of 60) had high-school or less education. Generally, one would expect the income of this level to be more represented in the under-$10,000 group. The fact that only 17 reported an income of under $10,000 leaves a group of 9 that could have been expected to be in this low-income group. The rest of the nonrespondents to income (ten) might be evenly distributed. Even if they were all in higher income groups, they would be offset by the nine supposed missing from the lower-income group. Therefore, the missing income data likely will tend toward the lower end, if at all, on the income scale. Any conclusions based on income data would have to consider that there is likely to be actually more income than is accounted for here. This reinforces the conclusions reached on these subhypotheses since the lower income trends are negative in subhypothesis A, negative in subhypothesis B, and positive in subhypothesis C.

Hypothesis IV

If certain problems and methods of financing exist, then homesteader satisfaction is affected.

In considering homesteader satisfaction or dissatisfaction, the assumption was made that when people have financial worries or concerns that interrupt their daily routines and pursuits or conflict with the people who cross their lives, they are dissatisfied with their life situation. We assumed that the financial problems that beset the homesteading program as well as the homesteaders, the problems of dealing with contractors and the problems of dealing with the myriad city agencies and bureaucracies, would create frustrations that would lower their perceptions of their own satisfactions. The hypothesis was divided into two subhypotheses, one relating to finance method and one relating to other problems, to see if there was a difference in the type of problems as they related to satisfaction.

Subhypothesis A. Satisfaction is affected by problems of the homesteaders.

Operational Terms

Satisfaction was operationalized by the following question: Are you satisfied with the homesteading program in your city? A great deal? Some? Not very much? Not at all? A great deal, some, not very much, and not at all became the scale for measuring the satisfaction level of homesteaders. These continuous values were the options given to the homesteader respondents.

Problems of homesteaders were listed in response to the following question: What problems related to homesteading did you need help in solving? This was an open-ended question. The answers were coded into three categories: personal problems, program problems, and neighborhood problems. These are the operational definition of problems of homesteaders.

TABLE 6.10

Homesteader Satisfaction as Related to Problem Identification

	Problems		
Satisfaction	Personal	Program	Neighborhood
A great deal			
Number	12	9	2
Percent	57	56	33
Some			
Number	8	4	3
Percent	38	25	50
Not very much			
Number	1	2	0
Percent	5	13	0
Not at all			
Number	0	1	1
Percent	0	6	17
Total responses*			
Number	21	16	6
Percent	100	100	100

*Multiple responses were given. They totaled 43 out of a possible 180 responses.

Source: Compiled by the authors.

Findings

We find that homesteaders had very few problems. The 60 homesteaders responding might possibly have recorded a total of 180 problems. Actually, only 43 problems were recorded. This is just 24 percent of the possible total. Only 21 of the 60 homesteaders had personal problems; only 6 of 60 had neighborhood problems that required help in solving. If other homesteaders had problems, they were not of sufficient magnitude to require assistance.

We can collapse the first two categories of satisfaction, a great deal and some, to denote satisfaction with the program. When we do this, we find that 20 of 21 homesteaders who had personal problems registered satisfaction with the program. We note that 13 of 16 homesteaders with program problems derived satisfaction with the program and that 5 of 6 homesteaders with neighborhood problems had satisfaction with the program. Neighborhood problems are the least significant. Only 10 percent of the homesteader respondents had neighborhood problems.

We assume that if a homesteader is satisfied not very much or not at all, then he is dissatisfied with the program. If we collapse the last 2 categories of satisfaction we find that only 5 problems of the total of 43 brought about dissatisfaction with the program.

Conclusion

We can conclude from these findings that the problems that needed help in solving were not of sufficient magnitude to cause dissatisfaction with the program. It is also possible that homesteaders were inured to the problems they encountered. Most people have personal problems related to housing. They have become so accustomed to dealing with them that they accept them as facts of life. Program problems usually denoted problems that resulted from the frustrations of dealing with the bureaucracies of city government and, although they may resent the time wasted and misunderstandings that result from lack of communication, they would not necessarily associate this type of frustration with homesteading specifically. Wayne King, who has written two articles for the New York Times on homesteading, cited the neighborhood problems in Baltimore as serious considerations that might affect the future of the program.[7] Our findings would tend to dispute his, considering the very few homesteaders who noted neighborhood or security problems.

Since satisfaction is very high in all categories of problems, we can conclude that problems are not important to a homesteader's

perception of satisfaction with the program. This subhypothesis is
not supported by the data.

Subhypothesis B. Satisfaction with the program is affected by the
finance method used by the homesteader.

We assumed that the finance method that a homesteader used
would affect his level of satisfaction because the different finance
methods had different interest rates, because the arrangements
required varying amounts of time and untangling of red tape, and
because using personal savings might engender resentments.

Operational Terms

Satisfaction is operationalized by the same question as in
subhypothesis IV-A: Are you satisfied with the homesteading program in your city? A great deal? Some? Not very much? Not at
all? Finance methods are operationalized as in subhypothesis III-B.
The type of financing refers to the loan procedure: conventional
loans, government loans, personal savings, and combinations of
outside loans with personal savings. Those respondents with
combinations were placed in the category of the outside loan
specified.

TABLE 6.11

Satisfaction with Program According to Finance Method

Satisfaction	Finance Method		
	Personal Savings	Conventional Loan	Government Loan
A great deal	9	8	21
Some	4	3	6
Not very much	2	1	1
Not at all	1	0	0
Total	16	12	28

Note: n = 60; not responding = 4.
Source: Compiled by the authors.

Findings

It seems that regardless of the finance method, homesteaders perceive satisfaction with the program. Of the 16 homesteaders who have used personal savings, 13 were satisfied. Of the 12 who used conventional loans, 11 were satisfied. Of the 28 who used some type of government loan, 27 were satisfied. The conventional loan users, who generally pay more interest than the government loan users, did not register less satisfaction with the program. Homesteaders who use personal savings seem to register slightly less satisfaction. These findings become more apparent when the first two categories are collapsed to denote satisfaction and when the last two categories are collapsed to denote dissatisfaction.

Conclusion

It was surprising to find that homesteaders who use personal savings and conventional loans did not register more dissatisfaction with the program. The possible explanation for this may be that the benefits of homesteading give so much satisfaction that the finance method is relatively unimportant. Additionally, there is the fact that a homestead applicant understands that he will have to find some source of financing when he applies for the program; therefore he anticipates the costs and other effects of borrowing money or using his own income or savings. The careful attention to this problem by the homestead officials probably has a great impact on the homesteaders. Applicants are given financial counseling in almost all homestead cities. Every effort is made to help the homesteader find the best loan source, to budget his income carefully, and to provide low-interest city loans if possible. The fact that almost half the homesteader respondents used city loans attests to this effort.

Since 81 percent of homesteaders who use personal savings are satisfied with the program, 92 percent of those who use conventional loans are satisfied, and 96 percent of those who use government loans are satisfied, we conclude that the method of financing is not related to satisfaction with the program. The hypothesis is not proved. A slightly higher percentage register satisfaction when loans are used rather than personal savings. Conversely, those who use personal savings register more dissatisfaction. However, this small percentage of dissatisfaction does not, in our opinion, affect the conclusion.

Since neither of the subhypotheses are supported by the data, Hypothesis IV is not proved. Homesteader satisfaction has little relation to the presence of certain problems or to the method of financing that homesteaders use. Subdividing the hypothesis did not reveal any difference between problems and finance method as each relates to satisfaction. We can conclude that satisfaction is related to other aspects of the program.

Hypothesis V

Homesteaders perceive greater stability in homestead neighborhoods than in their former neighborhoods.

One of the theories on which urban homesteading is based is the theory of neighborhood stability. Greater stability would be a first-order impact of the policy. Some of the factors that contribute to neighborhood stability are homeownership, percentage of abandoned properties, change in racial composition of the neighborhood, income level of the neighborhood, life-styles, social patterns, neighborhood interest, home maintenance, and appearance of the neighborhood. It is too soon to measure how homesteading affects many of these factors in homestead neighborhoods. However, this perception of the homesteaders about the homestead neighborhood can be a criterion measure since the attitude of the homesteader (or any resident) toward the neighborhood does affect the neighborhood stability.

TABLE 6.12

Homestead Neighborhoods as Perceived by Homesteaders

Variance from Former Neighborhood	Neighborhood Characteristics	
	Racial Integration	Neighborhood Interest
More		
Number	25	28
Percent	42	46
No difference		
Number	28	22
Percent	46	37
Less		
Number	7	10
Percent	12	17
Total		
Number	60	60
Percent	100	100

Note: n = 60.
Source: Compiled by the authors.

Operational Terms

Homesteader perception of neighborhood stability was based on questions of comparison about present and former neighbors and neighborhood. (See Appendix B, Homesteader Schedule.) The answers that indicated a change in the racial makeup and a change or difference in the amount of interest in the neighborhoods were operationalized to measure stability. When either factor was cited, we interpreted this to mean a difference between the amount of perceived stability in the homesteaders' present neighborhood and their former one.

Findings

The data gathered reflected the opinions of only those homesteaders who perceived change. We assumed those who did not perceive change saw no difference in the neighborhoods. They are included in the table. The number reporting a change is small. Only 32, or about 50 percent, of the 60 homesteader respondents perceived any change in racial integration. There were 38, or about 60 percent, who perceived a change in neighborhood interest. On the basis of the number who perceived changes only, 7 of 32 perceived less racial integration. Those 7 represent 22 percent of the 32 total. There were 26 percent of the respondents who perceived change in neighborhood interest who noted less interest in the homestead neighborhood (10 out of 38). Even when we leave out the nonrepondents ("no difference"), the percentage of homesteaders who perceived less interest and less integration remains relatively small. Most of the changes noted are in the direction of more rather than less neighborhood integration and more rather than less neighborhood interest. Almost half the homesteaders perceived no change in racial integration. A large percentage perceived no change in neighborhood interest. Since many homestead programs attempt to qualify applicants from the same or contiguous neighborhoods, we could expect a number to report no differences. Others who saw no difference may not have been in residence long enough to be aware of neighborhood interest.

Conclusion

We assume that more neighborhood interest and more integration are indications of perceived neighborhood stability. Since many respondents cited that their reason for homesteading was to help to restore the inner city, more integration would be a positive perception of stability. Inner-city neighborhoods are often characterized as increasingly black and disinterested. Those who sought to improve

the inner city by becoming homesteaders would look for greater
integration and greater neighborhood interest as indexes of stability.
On the basis of those who perceived change, the greatest percentage
perceived more integration and more neighborhood interest. This
finding would tend to prove the hypothesis. Since such a large number
of homesteaders perceived no change, we can conclude that the choice
of homestead neighborhoods by the city administrations is a factor
that needs to be considered. Program policy in many cities is to
select neighborhoods for homesteading that are only moderately
deteriorated—that have some measure of viability. This could account
for the large number of homesteaders who did not record a change.
Another factor could be homesteader selection. If homesteaders
previously lived nearby, they may perceive no change yet. It may
indeed be too soon to measure this first-order impact.

NOTES

1. U.S., Statutes at Large, vol. 63, 1949; U.S. Code, vols. 12,
42, 1970.
2. Jane Jacobs, Death and Life of Great American Cities (New
York: Vintage Books, 1961), p. 163.
3. James Davis, "The Urban Homestead Act," Landscape,
Winter 1970, p. 11.
4. Lewis Stone, "An Urban Homestead Act," Current, March
1973, p. 3.
5. Jane Jacobs, Death and Life, p. 163.
6. U.S. Bureau of the Census, 1970.
7. Wayne King, "Urban Homesteading Faltering in Fight against
Blight of Cities," New York Times, 30 May 1975, p. C 1.

CHAPTER

7

CONCLUSION

CITY ANALYSIS

We found that urban homesteading was a very complex concept. Legal and financial restrictions affected the program in every phase of its development. There was a multiplicity of participants whose perspectives differed widely. Politicians, bureaucrats, private-sector businessmen, and applicants were interrelated in every stage. There was also a multiplicity of decisions. These required the participation of many city departments interacting with each other and with the other participants. The multiple decisions required of the homesteaders complicated the process even further. Time was a major problem. The urgency of the problem dictated fast action. However, finding the solutions to the complex factors described above dictated delay.

Because of these difficulties of implementation, there could be little expectation of success. With so many complicating factors, urban homesteading seemed to be a doomed venture. Finding that urban homesteading was operating in a growing number of cities was surprising. Finding that urban homesteading was expanding in many of these cities was even more unexpected. Is there an explanation for this? Perhaps it is due to the fact that many cities included the plans for implementation in the policy definition. We found that most ordinances included specific regulations for the homesteader as well as for the city. These regulations dealt with the total home-steading period, not just the inception of the program. We also found administrative guidelines with equally detailed plans for implementation. Perhaps cities anticipated the needs of the applicants as well as the problems inherent in the program.

144

Goals

There are two goals that were emphasized most. One is directed toward improving the financial situation of the cities. This may have been stated as "improving the tax base" or "neighborhood preservation." The other goal is directed toward people: Homesteading helps meet the housing needs by rehabilitating the existing housing stock. This includes providing the opportunity for homeownership to those unable to obtain it otherwise.

If we could picture these two goals at either end of a scale, we would find few cities at the extremes. They tend to fall along the scale depending upon their own weighing of priorities. Regardless of their place on the scale, most cities use homesteading as a method for confronting their growing financial problems. Whether the program is promoted to provide upward mobility through homeownership or to increase the tax base, the financial situation of the city is eased. We conclude that urban homesteading is not only a housing program and a social program but that it is also an economic program. In Chapter 2 we discussed the role of a city's economic problems as motivating factors for adopting homesteading.

The effects of urban homesteading on the economy of a city cannot be measured until the program has been in existence for a number of years.

Administrative Structure

All homestead programs are locally initiated and directed. They are either part of an existing housing department or they operate as a separate agency. When the goals of the program tend toward the tax-improvement end of the scale, we find that the program may be in the tax department, licenses-and-inspection department, or in the city's real-estate division. When the goal of the program tends toward the homeownership end of the scale, we find the administration is often in community development or homeownership development departments. Programs that operate as separate agencies may be directed to either goal.

Program Implementation

Our descriptive analysis shows that the neighborhood, the house, and the homesteader must be economically viable in order to participate in the program. This holds true even when the stated goal of the program is socially oriented as in Philadelphia. In Philadelphia, we found that although the homeownership theory is the essence of the program, the city's economic problems intervened in program implementation.

The amount of support to the homesteader varies according to the program's stated goal. It is greater when the goal tends toward homeownership. In addition, more financial support and more special neighborhood programs are offered in these cities. Technical and personal support exist to some extent in all cities, regardless of the goal.

The older, eastern cities began the program first. There seems to be no common denominator in the histories or other unique characteristics of the cities. This could be due to the difficulty in identifying and in controlling the intervening variables that are present in each city. For instance, the income levels of homesteaders, amount of financial support, and cost of rehabilitation are all affected by the cost of living in that particular city.

STATISTICAL ANALYSIS

Civic Leaders

In all the cities included in our survey, civic leaders perceived the climate as receptive to urban homesteading. Business related to the housing industry was affected positively. Civic leaders tended to emphasize the social benefits to the homesteaders and the financial benefits to the city. There appears to be no problem in generating citizen support for an urban-homesteading policy. The media role in promoting urban homesteading seems to have been instrumental in developing positive citizen response. This should allay any fears public officials may have regarding public acceptance when they are considering institution or expansion of the program.

Officials

The surveys revealed that despite differences in administrative structure, there is similarity in the programs and the problems encountered. The number of abandoned houses affects the size of the program, except in Wilmington. The major problems are finances and time. These problems may not be peculiar to homesteading, however. Several other options for homesteading were supported by all officials. Some are in the experimental stage. This may

open the possibility for urban homesteading in some cities that do
not have large numbers of abandoned houses.

Homesteaders

Our data led us to believe that homesteading does not benefit
any specific segment of the society. Homesteaders are represented
across the broad spectrum of age, race, education, occupation, and
income. We can conclude from this that homesteading would be a
viable program in any community that has a stock of vacant, non-
productive housing or vacant land. It does not require any specific
type of citizen group to homestead these houses.

The problems encountered in homesteading do not seem to have
any bearing on the socioeconomic status of the homesteader. Homesteaders from every segment of the population had similar problems.
Therefore, homesteading should not pose any unique service problems
that a city could not anticipate from other programs in their own
city or in other cities.

Since we have discovered that higher-income whites are more
likely to homestead than higher-income blacks, it is very probable
that homesteading can bring about a degree of racial and economic
integration in the areas where it is instituted. This, in turn, may
lessen the possibility of abandonment which seems to feed on neighborhoods where low-income residents are concentrated.

SYNTHESIS

Cities

All the cities except Washington, D.C. have large numbers of
abandoned properties. The variety of mechanisms for acquiring the
property depends on the state statutory procedures. In some states
a fast simple procedure of transferral of the deed from owner to
purchaser (who holds a lien on the property by way of debts incurred
by the owner) involves a special court procedure. This avoids the
usual lengthy proceedings against the owner that allow increased
deterioration of the property. Lien preference is established by
state law and is administered by the judge before the property is transferred to the purchaser. In other states the city acquires the property
through tax delinquency after a waiting period of several years. Whether the city holds title to the property or the title is transferred in a
direct transaction to a new owner, the liens must be met. Unless
an owner has a free title, he may be unwilling to put the necessary

money into the rehabilitation of the dwelling. The acquisition costs
(covered in a rehabilitation loan) for a homesteader could include
a title search and payment of liens so as to assure a free title and
a new beginning for the property.

Financial mechanisms for loans as well as budget often begin
in the private sector. The joint venture (cooperation of private and
public sector) of making money available in the area referred to as
the "redlined district" assures wider community awareness of the
program. The money may be in the form of seed money to establish
a revolving fund for homesteaders with low-interest rates and long
terms or short terms with balloon payments and conventional refi-
nancing with the structure as collateral. It may be in the form of an
agreement to lend in the district with the city as guarantor of the
loan. Municipal bonds are used in several cities. These are justi-
fied as enabling abandoned structures to become tax paying.

Financial mechanisms for city acquisition of structures is another
problem. Since HUD structures are frequently numerous in inner-
city areas, use of these (especially VA and FHA mortgaged houses)
should be considered. HUD presently offers these for the lowest
residual value to the cities.

These various innovations in implementation indicate the broad
scope of interest, despite the program difficulties. Urban homesteading may in fact test the abilities of the smaller political juris-
dictions in the area of housing policies. The role of the federal
government has been limited thus far. The concept of urban homesteading emerged at a time when the federal government was transferring its support of urban programs to the cities. The Community
Development Act, with Section 810 on urban homesteading, could
result in increased federal support for the program.[1] Federal laws
and guidelines could eliminate many of the legal and financial restraints
that confront cities and states.

Program

The urban-homesteading concept as presently used is, for the
most part, based on the use of existing, abandoned housing stock.
Policy decision as to whether to preserve abandoned houses is
dependent on the alternatives available. Use of existing sound structures is claimed to be less expensive than building new housing by
every city involved in the program. The mechanisms and administration are somewhat complex, however. The use of vacant land is
Buffalo's approach to meeting the housing need and returning property
to the tax roll. Pittsburgh is using the concept to accomplish turnkey
ownership, which is a policy of selling title of a property to its renters

for the price of the rent. Renters of city-owned properties become homeowners as they rehabilitate their homes. This increases home-ownership and reduces the need for government maintenance. St. Louis homesteaders buy apartment houses of several units and rent out all the units but one to help finance the rehabilitation. Baltimore and St. Louis are experimenting with small-shop-and-house com-binations. New York's U-HAB has groups of citizens formed into corporations using their sweat equity to finance rehabilitation of apartment buildings.

New York's unique program is related to its very large stock of abandoned dwelling units (100,000 units in 7,000 buildings plus 2 or 3 additional buildings each day), much of which is structurally sound.[2] The city forecloses on the abandoned buildings and sells them to home-steaders. The sweat-equity program began in 1972. U-HAB was formed in 1974 to help meet the increasing interest and to offer more support services. Groups of tenants form corporations, acquire city-owned abandoned apartment buildings, and rehabilitate and manage them. The U-HAB staff provides legal assistance incorporating administra-tive assistance in organization of the project; assistance in location of a suitable structure; financial assistance with low-interest, long-term loans; and technical assistance with rehabilitation procedure (for sweat equity) and contract bids (for contracted work). The city allows a ten-year tax abatement. A tax abatement is a scale of reduced property taxes for a fixed period of time. Tax assessments are graduated or waived for several years in order to encourage investment in the homestead property. This sometimes requires legal changes. The rehabilitation loans are repaid to the city at a slightly higher interest rate (7 percent) than the city pays. The funds are made available through the sale of municipal bonds. A technical-assistance budget was established with seed money from banks, cor-porations, philanthropies, and the Episcopal diocese, cathedral, and parishes. The program is self-supporting.

Six building are now in the program, with 14 others in the applica-tion stage—a total of 20 buildings and 300 units. U-HAB's goal is to rehabilitate 200 abandoned buildings and 3,000 units in the next 2 years. The mortgage covers wages for some of the workers. Others live on welfare or part-time jobs for the 1-to-1 1/2 years needed for completion of the rehabilitation. U-HAB is investigating the possi-bilities of full-time employment in the construction trades for the owners of rehabilitated structures who have newly acquired skills in that area. Also, U-HAB plans to sponsor a retail, cooperative construction-materials store.

Other related programs in urban homesteading have included the neighborhood parks formed from vacant land transferred to a neighborhood corporation. Sometimes the land is used for community vegetable gardens, craft centers, or child-care centers.

Problems

It appears that it does not matter whether homesteading is administered as a separate city program or as part of another agency or agencies. Problems and successes are recorded in both approaches. The determination and positive program of the staff and the homesteaders seem to be the important value.

Citizen leaders have testified to the fact that the climate in the city is very hospitable to homesteading. Additionally, there is evidence from them that homesteading may help present businesses and could possibly restore businesses that have left deteriorating neighborhoods.

Homesteading seems to be forcing cities to reevaluate their property-tax laws. Whereas it has been recognized for some time that present tax laws penalize the citizen who attempts to maintain his property and reward the one who does not, it has taken the homesteading experience to bring this point out.

Cities have encountered complicated problems in the area of acquisition of stock. Shortening the foreclosure time so that houses can be turned over before they are beyond repair has legal implications that have not yet been tested. Many cities are constrained legally from the "giving" of these houses. Those who do not have this limitation may yet find that giving away houses is outside the law. The use for homesteading of cleared inner-city land that has been acquired through eminent domain has also to be tested in the courts. Buffalo is working in this area and may provide the legal guidelines for this type of homesteading. The cities that are bypassing this method of acquisition and seeking instead to buy their stock from FHA foreclosures or from HUD need a financial reservoir for this purpose. This type of procedure may intervene in the abandonment process but it does not confront the current problem of already abandoned or deteriorated units.

Another problem not yet confronted is the owner-equity problem. Since most homesteads are in economically marginal neighborhoods, there may be a need to provide equity insurance. Many of the problems are related to financing. Perhaps this is because the program is undertaken as a housing policy rather than an economic policy. In assessing the need for the program, the emphasis has been only on costs of acquisition of houses and not the costs of implementation of the program, also.

Benefits

There are two types of benefits: financial and social. The city's financial returns are seen in increased taxes. Social returns are seen in increased homeownership, neighborhood stability, and more positive perceptions of the city. Several of the city officials noted the value of social benefits; all the civic leaders noted social benefits. A large proportion of homesteaders noted social benefits.

Homeownership is valued by the homesteaders in our survey as the primary benefit of homesteading. Since homesteaders can be said to represent a sample, or cross section, of a total citizen group, homeownership emerges as a value of our society. Regardless of the specific goal a city may have for its homesteading program, it is achieved through providing homeownership. In this way homesteading is satisfying a very real need of our society.

We still do not know if sweat equity pays off. There is much apprehension regarding this. However, although the homesteads cannot legally be turned over until the period of the living agreement is fulfilled, some of them have already been assessed at two or three times the total of the original value plus the rehabilitation costs. (Our Washington interviews revealed some startling figures of this type.) The selection of the neighborhood for homesteading becomes an important factor in the eventual value of homesteads.

All officials agreed that urban homesteading cannot be considered a panacea. It should be viewed as a catalyst. The effects of urban homesteading are not only reflected in homesteaders and in homesteads. The effects of increased neighborhood activity, insofar as there has been renovation to other houses not in the program, have been identified by several officials and civic leaders. This catalytic effect was anticipated as a second-order impact in many cities.

IMPLICATIONS

One of the problems that many government programs encounter is the expectation of early positive returns. We have tried to allow for the newness of the program in our own analysis. There is ample need for further study now and for planning future studies as well. We suggest 2 areas for further study: policy implementation research and policy evaluation research. A brief description of each is given here.

Policy Implementation Research

We propose research into the area of implementation based upon models. This should clarify and aid in the understanding of how homesteading works now and how it could work better.

A model could be developed based on the goal-orientation scale discussed earlier in this chapter. The various weights assigned by cities to their priorities could be measured by their position on the scale. These weights would indicate model types.

An analysis of the administration and programs could lead to the formulation of models. These models could then be used for prediction of success of any program designed for general city application (not for a specific benefit group). Possible models that seem applicable are in goal-orientations, in the homestead board (policy-making group), in the administration of the program, and in the selection process used for homesteaders.

Models of homestead boards could be in the form of government-dominated membership (city officials and public-administration professionals), professional-dominated membership (bankers, lawyers, real-estate interests, contractors), and government-professional-citizen membership (a balanced board of representatives of each category). The models seem to exist in the cities surveyed. The relationship between a particular model and the goals of the city would be a subject for future study.

The administration vehicles fall into five categories or models: tax-collection departments, community-development departments, real-estate land banks, redevelopment-and-housing authorities, and separate agencies directly responsible to the principal administrator or the city. The selection of a particular vehicle for the administration of the program is possibly related to the goals of the city.

Models for the selection process are of three types: citizens qualify as potential homesteaders, bid, and are approved by the city council; properties qualify as homestead sites, applications are received by the administrative office, and a lottery is held; and properties qualify as homestead sites, applications are received, and an in-house selection of homesteaders is made.

The choices made by each city as to the type of model in each area may reflect the environment of that particular city.

Policy Evaluation Research

We propose an evaluation impact study for future use. This study would be based on goal orientation. The study might be designed as an ex post facto model with matched controls at three points in time. In order to achieve matched controls, we suggest using the programs whose goals are at opposite ends of the goal orientation scale. St. Louis, Missouri and Philadelphia, Pennsylvania occupy such positions. These two cities have similar-sized housing stock available and have similar-sized programs. The study would show the impact of the program in cities with different goals. The primary and secondary impacts would be measured at three specific times:

when homesteaders complete residency requirements; at the end of
the average length of residence for the city (as recorded in city
census data); and ten years after the program's inception. We
believe measures at these points in time will provide insight into
the impact of the policy on urban housing markets.

The study should include the following:

I. First-order impacts
   A. Improved tax base—from city records
   B. Neighborhood stability in homestead neighborhoods
      1. Homeownership rates—from census data
      2. Average length of residence—from census data
      3. Rates of abandonment—from census data
      4. Homesteader's equity—from city deed recordings and
         homestead office records
      5. Homestead property maintenance—from city tax assessor
         and inspection departments
II. Second-order impacts
   A. Changes in socioeconomic status of homesteaders—from
      homesteader survey
   B. Changes in socioeconomic status of neighbors—from census
      data
   C. Property maintenance of neighborhood—from collection and
      inspection departments
   D. Changes in city services—from various city departments
      (fire calls, police calls, public relations programs)
   E. Changes in activities of neighborhood groups—from neighbor-
      hood citizen survey
   F. Changes in business activity—from tax collector
   G. Changes in stability in contiguous neighborhoods—measured
      by same methods as first-order impacts
   H. Changes in lending policies of financial institutions—from
      those institutions' records
   I. Changes in program—from homestead office

Intervening variables that might affect the program should be
considered. These could include changes in homestead emphasis or
size; legal changes that affect funding or housing stock; transportation policies of city, region, or state; changes in resources (energy
or industry); and land-use policies.

NOTES

1. U.S. Congress, House, Housing and Community Development Act of 1974, 93rd Cong., 2nd sess., 1974, p. 101.

2. U.S. Department of Housing and Urban Development, Office of Policy Development and Research, Neighborhood Preservation: A Catalog of Local Programs (Washington, D.C.: U.S. Government Printing Office, February 1975), pp. 161-62.

APPENDIX A
STAGES OF URBAN
HOMESTEADING PROGRAMS

Established
  Baltimore, Md.
  Buffalo, N.Y.
  Camden, N.J.
  Dayton, Oh. [c]
  Minneapolis, Minn.
  Newark, N.J.
  New York City, N.Y. [b]
  Philadelphia, Pa.
  Pittsburgh, Pa.
  Rockford, Ill.
  St. Louis, Mo.
  Washington, D.C.
  Wilmington, Del.
Developing
  Atlanta, Ga.
  Columbus, Oh.
  Detroit, Mich.
  New Orleans, La.
  Pomona, Cal.
  Providence, R.I.
  Seattle, Wash.

Abandoned Local Plan
  Cincinnati, Oh.
  Houston, Tex.
  Oakland, Calif.
HUD Sec. 810[a] Participants
  Atlanta, Ga.
  Baltimore, Md.
  Boston, Mass.
  Chicago, Ill.
  Cincinnati, Oh.
  Columbus, Oh.
  Dallas, Tex.
  Decatur, Ga.
  Gary, Ind.
  Indianapolis, Ind.
  Islip, N.Y.
  Jersey City, N.J.
  Kansas City, Mo.
  Minneapolis, Minn.
  New York City, N.Y.
  Oakland, Calif.
  Philadelphia, Pa.
  Rockford, Ill.
  South Bend, Ind.
  Tacoma, Wash.
  Wilmington, Del.

---

[a] U.S. Department of Housing and Urban Development, HUD News, 10 October 1975, pp. 3-6.

[b] Discovered while study in progress. Findings in Conclusion, Chapter 7.

[c] Discovered while study in progress. Findings in city comparisons table, Chapter 5.

CIVIC-LEADER SCHEDULE

There is a program in your city for rehabilitating abandoned homes and providing home ownership through urban homesteading. This concept is currently being considered by many other cities. We would appreciate your help in evaluating the program.

This information will be held in strict confidence. It will be used, without identification, for data processing only.

1. Do you think Homesteading is beneficial to your city?
   □ Yes   □ No   □ Don't know
   a.   If yes, how does it benefit the city?
         Financially:
                 □ (1) Improved tax base
                 □ (2) Help city
                 □ (3) Help private business
                 □ (4) Other (please specify) _____
         Socially:
                 □ (1) Helps meet local housing needs
                 □ (2) Provides opportunities for citizens
                 □ (3) Improves neighborhood stability
                 □ (4) Improves citizen attitudes
                 □ (5) Other (please specify) _____
         Cosmetically:
                 □ (1) Improves appearance of city
                 □ (2) Discourages vandalism
                 □ (3) Other (please specify) _____

2. Has Homesteading encouraged other citizens to maintain or improve their homes?
   □ Yes   □ No   □ Don't know

3. Has Homesteading caused real-estate values to change in neighborhoods where it exists?
   □ Yes   □ No   □ Don't know
   a.   If "yes," how?   Raised values   Lowered values

4. Do you think Homesteading will prevent further neighborhood abandonment and deterioration?
   □ Yes   □ No   □ Don't know

5. Has Homesteading affected your business in any way?
   □ Yes   □ No   □ Don't know
   a.   If "yes, " How? _____

6. Has Homesteading affected other businesses that you know of?
   □ Yes   □ No   □ Don't know
   a.   If "yes, " would you specify? _____

7. Are you aware of any citizen opposition to the program?
   □ Yes   □ No   □ Don't know
   a.   If "yes, " please explain. _____

8. What is your occupation? _____

9. Would you recommend Homesteading to other cities who may
   be considering the program?
   □ Yes   □ No   □ Don't know

10. Would you suggest any changes in the program for your city or
    others?
    □ Yes   □ No
    a.   If "yes, " please explain. _____

HOMESTEADING-OFFICIAL SCHEDULE — LONG FORM

1. Name of City _____

2. Population of City as of 197_____

3. What type of government structure do you have?
   □ council/manager
   □ mayor/council

4. What type of elections do you have?   □ partisan   □ non-partisan

5. What is the name of the Urban Homesteading program in your
   city? _____

6. Is the Urban Homesteading Program a separate program or part
   of an established housing agency?   □ separate
   □ part of another agency (housing)

7. Are the services and personnel available to Homesteaders shared
   by other programs?   □ yes   □ no, they are separate

8.   How many people have been assigned on a fulltime basis to the Urban Homesteading Program? _____
      a.   How many on a part time basis? _____

9. When did your city adopt Urban Homesteading? _____

10. Was a local ordinance on Urban Homesteading passed by the city government?   □ Yes   □ No

11.   Does the city authorize basic rehabilitation on the houses before transferring them to Homesteaders?   □ Yes   □ No

      Explain, if necessary. _____

12. In many cities, other legal changes had to be made in order to have Urban Homesteading. In your city, were any changes made in the City Charter?   · □ Yes   □ No
      □ a.   If "yes," were changes made in deferral of real estate taxes upon Homesteaders?
      □ b.   If, "yes", were housing-code allowances given Homesteaders during rehabilitation period?
      □ c.   If "yes", were changes made in process of acquisition of abandoned homes?
      d.   Was an enabling clause by the state legislature necessary?   □ Yes   □ No
      e.   What other changes in the local legal framework were made?
      _____

13.   Does your city use a Federal act, such as the Community Development Urban Homestead Act (Section 810) or a Federally funded program to implement the Urban Homesteading Program?   □ Yes   □ No
      a.   Which one(s)? _____

14.   Who legally holds the title to the property during Homesteading? _____

15.   What is your legal definition of "abandoned house" in connection with Homesteading in your city? _____
      a.   How many houses are abandoned, using this definition, in your city? _____

16.   What are the foreclosure procedures used for homes that might be involved in the Urban Homesteading program?
      _____

17. What criteria are used in selecting the specific homes for the program? _____

18. Approximately how many homes are available for Homesteading in your city? _____

19. How many homes are in the program? _____

20. What are the values of these homes and their estimated rehabilitation costs? (Please list on reverse side of this sheet)

21. Are these homes   □ clustered in a few neighborhoods?
                        □ scattered through the city
                        □ both
     a.   How many neighborhoods are affected? _____

22. What is the maximum number of homes that your city eventually plans to have in the Homesteading program? _____

23. Are any of the Homesteading areas zoned for, or do they have variances for anything other than residential use? □ Yes   □ No
     Please explain if necessary. _____

24. When do Homesteads become tax-producing in your city? _____

25. Is the assessment graduated? □ Yes   □ No
     a.   If "yes", for what period of time? _____

26. What will be the annual tax benefits received by the city when the Homesteading program meets your present projection?

     _____

27. What is the dollar cost of the program to the city? (Please itemize in general categories, such as salaries, service delivery, tax abatement, etc.) _____

28. How many citizens have applied to be Homesteaders? _____
     a.   In selecting Homesteaders, what special qualities or skills are given priorities? _____
     b.   Are area residents given priority for a home in their area? □ Yes   □ No
     c.   In your opinion, what income level benefits most from the program? (check all that apply)
          □ under $10,000   □ $10,000 - $14,999
          □ $15,000 - 19,999   □ $20,000 - $29,999
          □ over $30,000

    d.   What have you done to make citizens aware of the Home-
steading program? _____

29.   What sources of loan funds are available to Homesteaders for
rehabilitation? _____
    a.   What are the interest rates, generally? _____
    b.   What are the loan terms, generally? _____
    c.   Does the city guarantee the loans for the Homesteaders?
        □ Yes   □ No

30.   How many Homesteaders have left the program? _____
    □ a.   For financial reasons?
    □ b.   For other reasons? Please specify. _____

31.   Please list the services which are offered through the Urban
Homesteading program. _____
    a.   Are these services utilized?
        □ not at all   □ not very much   □ some   □ a great deal
        (Please place each service in one of the above categories.)
    b.   Are these services organized separately under the Home-
steading program or are they part of existing city services?
        □ Organized separately   □ Part of existing city services
        (Please place each service in one of the above categories.)
    c.   Are additional regular city services required in the Home-
steading area?   □ Yes   □ No
        Please explain, if necessary. _____

32.   What major problems have been encountered with the program?
_____
    a.   How were they solved? _____

33.   What unexpected benefits have come from the program, such as
skill development of Homesteaders, improved neighborhoods,
participation by other citizens from other areas of city?
_____

34.   What are the long-term goals of Homesteading in your city?
_____

35.   What are the short-term goals of Homesteading in your city?
_____

36.   How successful do you feel that Homesteading has been in your
city?   □ very successful   □ somewhat successful
        □ not very successful   □ unsuccessful

37. Is there anything unique about this city that makes Homesteading especially useful? _____

38. What other rehabilitation programs are operating in your city at present? _____

39. In your opinion could the Homesteading principle be used in your city in these areas?

	Don't know	Yes	No	Maybe
Commercial property				
Multi-family units				
Vacant land				

40. Do you have any comments or suggestions or additional information that would be helpful in evaluating the Homesteading program in your city? _____

Please include any printed material relevant to these questions or descriptive of other aspects of the Homesteading program.

HOMESTEADING-OFFICIAL SCHEDULE — SHORT FORM

1. How successful do you feel that Homesteading has been in your city? □ very successful   □ somewhat successful   □ not very successful   □ unsuccessful

2. Is there anything unique about your city that makes Homesteading especially useful? _____

3. What are the long-term goals of Homesteading in your city?

   _____

4. What are the short-term goals of Homesteading in your city?

   _____

5. What unexpected benefits have come from the program? (i. e. new skills for Homesteaders, participation by citizens from other parts of city, etc.) _____

6. What major problems have been encountered with the program?

   _____

   a. How were they solved? _____

7. Do the Homesteaders utilize the support services which the Homesteading program offers them?
   □ a great deal   □ some   □ not very much   □ not at all
   (Please place each service in one of the above categories.)

8. In your opinion, could the Homesteading principle be used in your city in these areas?

	Don't know	Yes	No	Maybe
Commercial property				
Multi-family units				
Vacant land				

9. Do you have any comments or suggestions or additional information that would be helpful in evaluating the Homesteading program in your city?

HOMESTEADER SCHEDULE

TO BE FILLED IN BY THE HOMESTEADER. All personal information will be strictly confidential and will be used for data processing only, without names or identification.

_____
Name of City

1. Address _____

2. Is this your first home to own?   □ Yes   □ No

3. How many people are living in your home? _____

4. Number of children living at home. _____

5. How long did you live in your last home? _____

6. In your last home, what was your monthly rent or mortgage payment? _____
   a.   Did this include utilities?   □ Yes   □ No

7. In what city was your last home? _____
   a.   In what neighborhood? (Give nearest intersection if that describes the neighborhood more closely) _____

b.   Is this new location more convenient for transportation?
      □ Yes   □ No

8. Are your present neighbors similar to your former neighbors?
    □ Yes, the same   □ Some difference   □ No, very different
    a.   If you answered "some difference" or "very different,"
          how are they different? (check all that apply)
          □ More children in present neighborhood
          □ More old people in present neighborhood
          □ More integration in present neighborhood
          □ Less integration in present neighborhood
          □ Residents more interested in this neighborhood
          □ Residents less interested in this neighborhood
          □ Other (please specify) _____
    b.   Which neighborhood do you like better?
          □ Present neighborhood
          □ Former neighborhood
          □ Equally

9. Does this neighborhood appear to be better than your former
    one?   □ Yes   □ No
    a.   If you said "yes," how is it better?
          □ Present neighborhood cleaner
          □ Present neighborhood houses in better repair
          □ Crime less in present neighborhood
          □ Schools better in present neighborhood
          □ Other (please specify) _____

10. Without Homesteading, would you have attempted to buy a home?
    □ Yes   □ No
    a.   If "no", why not? _____

11. How long have you been a Homesteader? _____

12. People have different reasons for wanting to Homestead. What
    was your reason for applying to the Homestead program?
    _____

13. Have you had any contact with other Homesteaders through a
    Homesteading or neighborhood organization?   □ Yes   □ No

14. What special skills or resources do you have that will help or
    have helped you in the renovation of your house?
          □ carpentry
          □ electrical ability

☐ knowledge of plumbing
☐ money for rehabilitation
☐ other (please specify) _____

15. How well have you been satisfied with the Homesteading program?
☐ a great deal   ☐ some   ☐ not very much   ☐ not at all
   a. What parts of the program have been especially helpful?
   _____
   b. What problems related to Homesteading did you need
      help in solving? _____
   c. What are the benefits that you have had from Homesteading?
   _____
   d. Have you found the support services adequate?
      ☐ Yes   ☐ No

16. What method of financing are you using for the rehabilitation
    work?
      ☐ conventional bank loan
      ☐ city government loan
      ☐ agency loan (specify) _____

17. Please check the appropriate boxes below describing yourself.
   a. ☐ male   ☐ female
   b. Age: ☐ under 30   ☐ 31-40   ☐ 41-50   ☐ 51 or older
   c. ☐ married   ☐ single   ☐ widowed   ☐ divorced
   d. Race: ☐ black   ☐ white   ☐ other (please specify) _____
   e. Ethnic group: ☐ Anglo   ☐ Mexican   ☐ Puerto Rican
      ☐ Other (please specify) _____

18. What is your occupation? _____
   a. List any other employed persons and their occupations
      who live in this household. (Please give relationship to
      you, not names.) _____

19. What was the last grade that you completed in school? _____
   a. List any other adults in the household by their relationship
      to you and give their last grade completed. _____

20. What do you expect the total take home pay for this household to
    be for 1975? _____

21. We are studying how well Homesteading is working so that other
    cities can learn of it. Would you recommend Homesteading to
    other citizens?   ☐ Yes   ☐ No
   a. If not, why not? _____

22.   What recommendations would you make to your city for improving
      the program? _____

23.   What suggestions would you give to other citizens who plan to
      become Homesteaders? _____

      Thank you for your time and help. Please return as soon as
possible in the envelope enclosed.

LEGAL DOCUMENTS, BILLS, HEARINGS

Camden City Council. "An Ordinance to Promote the Utilization of Existing Housing." Administrative Code, Ordinance MC-894. Camden, N.J.: 29 November 1974. Mimeographed.

Pennsylvania State Legislature. "Hearings on Pennsylvania House Bill No. 1703." Presented to Pennsylvania State Legislature in 1974 by City of Pittsburgh. Mimeographed.

Rockford City Council. An Amendment to the City of Rockford Homestead Ordinance. 1974. Mimeographed.

U.S. Congress, House. A Bill to Establish a National Homestead Program: H.R. 10926. 93rd Cong., 1st sess., 1973, pp. 1-6.

_____.Committee on Banking and Currency. Subcommittee on Housing. Housing and Community Development: Hearings on H.R. 12197. 93rd Cong., 1st sess., 1973, p. 1957.

_____.Committee on the District of Columbia. Subcommittee on the Judiciary. Urban Homesteading: Hearings on H.R. 12197. 93rd Cong., 2nd sess., 1974.

_____.Congressional Record, 93rd Cong., 1st sess., 1973, 119, H 5935. (Congresswoman Holt speaking for urban Homesteading, 11 July 1973.)

_____.Congressional Record, 93rd Cong., 1st sess., 1973, 119, E 5888. (Congresswoman Holt speaking on federal housing programs, 19 September 1973.)

_____.Housing and Community Development Act of 1974. 93rd Cong., 2d sess., 1974, pp. 101-02.

_____.Housing and Urban Development Act of 1968: Public Law 90-448. 90th Cong., 2nd sess., 1968.

U.S. Congress, Senate. Committee on Banking, Housing and Urban Affairs. Hearings on Housing and Community Development: S.R. 3066. 93rd Cong., 1st sess., 1974, p. 48.

_____.Congressional Record, 93rd Cong., 1st sess., 1973, 119, part 28: 36487-90. (Senator Biden speaking for the Urban Homestead Act.)

U.S. Statutes at Large, vol. 5. 1856. (Armed Occupation Act.)

_____.Statutes at Large, vol. 12. 1862. (Morrill Act.)

_____.Statutes at Large, vol. 12. 1863. (Rural Homestead Act.)

_____.Statutes at Large, vol. 63. 1949. U.S. Code, vols. 12, 42. 1970. (Housing Act of 1949.)

_____.Statutes at Large, vol. 68. 1954. U.S. Code, vols. 12, 18, 20, 31, 38, 40, 42. 1970. (Housing Act of 1954.)

_____.Statutes at Large, vol. 75. 1961. U.S. Code, vols. 12, 15, 40, 42. 1970. (Housing Act of 1961.)

_____.Statutes at Large, vol. 78. 1964. U.S. Code, vols. 12, 15, 20, 38, 40, 42, 49. 1970. (Housing Act of 1965.)

_____.Statutes at Large, vol. 80. 1966. U.S. Code, vol. 12. 1970. (Housing Act of 1965, Amend. P.L. 89-754, Model Cities Act, Title X.)

Wilmington City Council. "Agreement between City of Wilmington and Several Commercial Banks and Lending Corporations." Administrative Code. Wilmington Del.: 12 May 1973.

_____."Ordinance Amending Chapter 33A Homestead Program. Administrative Code. Wilmington, Del.: 3 May 1973.

_____."An Ordinance Amending the City Code by Adding a New Chapter 33A Entitled 'Homestead Program.'" Administrative Code. Wilmington, Del.: 17 May 1973.

_____."Ordinance to Grant a Partial Tax Exemption." Administrative Code. Wilmington, Del.: 21 August 1972.

GOVERNMENT PUBLICATIONS

Federal

Armstrong, James E. "Rehabilitation, Conservation, Preservation."
    HUD Challenge, March 1973, pp. 2-5.

Baltimore Department of Housing and Community Development.
    "Homesteading." In The Settler. Baltimore, Md.: City Fair Edi-
    tion, 1974.

Berry Mary F. "Homesteading New Prescription for Urban Ills."
    HUD Challenge, January 1974, pp. 2-5.

Holt, Marjorie, Congresswoman. News release, 27 September 1973.

_____. News release, 22 May 1975.

"More Eligible for HUD Houses." Housing and Urban Affairs Daily,
    17 June 1975, p. 155.

"Philadelphia Awards First Houses to Urban Homesteaders." HUD
    Challenge, September 1974, p. 15.

Sternlieb, George. "Toward an Urban Homestead Act." In Hearings
    of the Committee on Banking and Currency. Washington, D.C.:
    Government Printing Office, 1971.

U.S. Department of Housing and Urban Development. Abandoned
    Housing Research: A Compendium. Washington, D.C.: U.S.
    Department of Housing and Urban Development, 1973.

_____. "'Homesteading' in Cities Suggested by HUD Official." HUD
    News, 21 October 1972.

_____. HUD News, 23 June 1975.

_____. HUD News, 10 October 1975.

_____. Invitation to Participate in an Urban Homesteading Demonstra-
    tion. Unpublished document.

_____. Preliminary Urban Homesteading Plan, for Discussion Purposes.
    Unpublished document. June 1975.

____."Urban Homestead Program Start Depends on Solving Legal
Riddles." Housing and Urban Development Trends 74-39.

____. Bureau of Land Management. Homesteading Past and Present.
Washington, D.C.: U.S. Government Printing Office, December
1973.

____.Office of Policy Development and Research. Neighborhood
Preservation: A Catalog of Local Programs. Washington, D.C.:
U.S. Government Printing Office, February 1975.

State

California Senate, Committee on Government Organization. Urban
Homesteading: Sweat Equity at Work Helping to Solve the Housing
Problems. Mimeographed. Sacramento, Calif.: 4 December 1974.

Rother, Steven C. "Urban Homesteading: It May Be One Way to Reclaim
Abandoned City Dwellings." New Jersey Municipalities, January
1974, pp. 14-17.

Local

Backers, Joseph J. The Land Reutilization Story. St. Louis, Mo.:
Land Reutilization Authority, 2 January 1974.

Baltimore Department of Housing and Community Development.
Homesteading. Baltimore, Md.: April 1975. (Report on first year
of homesteading in Baltimore.)

____. The Settler. Baltimore, Md.: May 1975.

Camden City Council. "Purposes of Homesteading." In Administrative
Guidelines. Camden, N.J.: 1974.

City of Baltimore. Home Rehabilitation, How to Start It, How to
Finish It, How to Manage It. Baltimore, Md.: July 1974.

Coleman, Joseph. "Philadelphia Urban Homestead Program: A Report
on the First Year of Funded Operation." Unpublished report.

Columbus Department of Development. "An Analysis of Community
Improvement Tools for Columbus, Ohio." Columbus, Ohio:
28 May 1974.

Minneapolis Housing and Redevelopment Authority. "Applications
for the Three Homes." Minneapolis, Minn.: 28 April 1975.

_____. Low Interest Loans and Grants, City of Minneapolis: Adminis-
trative Guidelines. Minneapolis, Minn.: 1974.

_____. Minneapolis Urban Homesteading: Administrative Guidelines.
Minneapolis, Minn.: 7 November 1974.

_____. "Profile of Applicants in First Lottery." Minneapolis, Minn.:
17 December 1974.

O'Laughlin, David L., Housing Coordinator. "Letter to Prospective
Homesteaders." Pittsburgh, Pa.

The Philadelphia Partnership. "Urban Homesteading: A Status Report."
Unpublished report. Philadelphia, Pa.: November 1974.

Philadelphia Urban Homestead Office. "The Facts about Urban Homesteading." Unpublished brochure. Philadelphia, Pa.

_____. "Philadelphia Urban Homestead Program." Unpublished report.
Philadelphia, Pa.: 22 November 1974.

Pittsburgh City Council. City Urban Homesteading Program: Legis-
lative Hearings. Pittsburgh, Pa.: 14 February 1974. (Held at
10:00 A.M. in city council chambers.)

Rockford Department of Community Renewal. "Urban Homesteading
in Rockford." Mimeographed. Rockford, Ill.: 1975.

St. Louis Land Reutilization Authority. "The St. Louis Plan of
Urban Homesteading." St. Louis, Mo: 2 January 1974.

Urban Homestead Board. "Homestead as an Option." Mimeographed.
Wilmington, Del.

_____. "Regulations of the Wilmington Homestead Board." Pamphlet.
Wilmington, Del.: 1 May 1974.

_____. "The Wilmington Homestead Program." Unpublished report.
Wilmington, Del.: 1974.

SCHOLARLY REPORTS AND ORIGINAL RESEARCH

Abrahamson, Julia. A Neighborhood Finds Itself. New York: Harper
and Bros., 1959.

Abrams, Charles. Home Ownership for the Poor. New York: Praeger,
1970.

Akre, M. Jan. "Urban Homesteading: Once More Down the Yellow
Brick Road." Environmental Affairs 3, no. 3 (1974): 563-94.

Benson, Charles S., and Lund, Peter B. Neighborhood Distribution
of Local Public Service. Berkeley: University of California,
Institute of Government Studies, 1969.

Bilyk, Andrej. "Savoring a City's Ethnic Flavor." Nation's Cities,
November 1973, 14-16.

"Calculating Urban Homestead Exemptions: A Proportionate Increase
Theory." Houston Law Review 11 (January 1974): 491-99.

Case, Frederick E. Inner City Housing and Private Enterprise.
New York: Praeger, 1972.

Chamberlain, G.U. "Homesteading Offers Antidote for Urban Blight."
American City 89 (January 1974): 60.

Clawson, Marion. "Urban Renewal in 2000." Journal of American
Institute of Planners, May 1968, pp. 173-9.

Coleman, Joseph E., Esq. "Urban Homesteading: A Plan for Developing Our New Frontiers." Paper presented to the Philadelphia
Planning Commission, 1968.

"Comments: Philadelphia's Urban Homesteading Ordinance: A Poor
Beginning toward Reoccupying the Urban Ghost Town." Buffalo
Law Review 23, no. 3 (Spring 1974): 735-63.

Crothers, R.J. "Factors Related to the Community Index of Satis-
factoriness." Ekistics 30 (August 1970): 107-09.

Davis, James H. "A Second Look at the Urban Homestead." Landscape,
January 1975, pp. 23-27.

_____. "The Urban Homestead Act." Landscape, Winter 1970, pp. 11-23.

Drewes, W. Chris. "Homesteading 1974: Reclaiming Abandoned Houses on the Urban Frontier." Columbia Journal of Law and Social Problems 10 (Spring 1974): 416-55.

Douglas Committee. "Urban Housing Needs through the 1980's: An Analysis and Projection." Research Report no. 10, 1968. (Prepared for the National Commission on Urban Problems.)

Edwards, Gordon. Land, People and Policy. West Trenton, N.J.: Chandler-Davis Publishing Co., 1969.

Fried, Edward R.; Rivlia, Alice M.; Schultz, Charles L.; and Teeters, Nancy H. Setting National Priorities: The 1974 Budget. Washington, D.C.: Brookings Institution, 1973.

Fried, Marc, and Gleicher, Peggy. "Some Sources of Residential Satisfaction in an Urban Slum." Journal of American Institute of Planners 27 (November 1961): 305-15.

"From Plows to Pliers: Urban Homesteading in America." The Fordham Urban Law Journal 2 (Winter 1974): 273-304.

Gans, Herbert J. "Heterogeneity and Homogeneity in Residential Areas—the Balanced Community." Journal of American Institute of Planners 27 (August 1961): 176-84.

Grier, George, and Grier, Eunice. Equality and Beyond. Chicago: Quadrangle Books, 1966.

Hooper, Willian L. "Innovation in Housing: Pipe Dreams or Practical Reality." Technology Review 70, no. 3 (January 1968): 25-31.

Jacobs, Jane. Death and Life of Great American Cities. New York: Vintage Books, 1961.

Kasarda, John D. "The Impact of Suburban Population Growth on Central City Service Function." American Journal of Sociology 77, no. 6 (May 1972): 1111-24.

Kurzman, Paul A., ed. The Mississippi Experience. New York: Associated Press, 1971.

Love v. Hoffman, 499 SW2d 295 (1973).

Luebbers, Thomas A. "Guidelines for Urban Homesteading." Municipal Attorney 15, no. 3 (March 1974): 75, 95.

McKenzie, Roderick Duncan. The Neighborhood: A Study of Local Life in the City of Columbus, Ohio. Chicago: University of Chicago Press, 1970.

Mandzak, Linda Joy. "A Cost-Benefit Analysis of the Baltimore Urban Scattered-Site Homestead Program." Baltimore, Md: May 1975.

Millspaugh, Martin, and Breckenfeld, Gurney. The Human Side of Urban Renewal. New York: Ives Washburn: 1960.

Molotch, Harvey. "Racial Change in a Stable Community." American Journal of Sociology 75, no. 2 (September 1969): 226-38.

National Urban Coalition. Urban Homesteading: Process and Potential. Washington, D.C.: National Urban Coalition, January 1974.

Ottoson, Howard W. Land Use Policy and Problems in the U.S. Lincoln, Neb.: University of Nebraska, 1963.

Page, Alfred N. Urban Analysis, Glenview, Ill.: Scott Forsman and Co., 1972.

"Property Abandonment in Detroit." Wayne Law Review 20, no. 3 (March 1974): 845-88.

Rasmussen, David. Urban Economics. New York: Harper and Row, 1973.

"Rehabilitation on Scattered Public Housing Sites May Help Save Wilmington, Delaware Neighborhoods." Journal of Housing, February 1975, pp. 78-79.

Rosenfeld, Raymond. Unpublished data collected for a study of Colonial Place, Norfolk, Virginia. Summer 1975.

"St. Louis Homestead Plan Now Entering Second Year." Journal of Housing, May 1974, pp. 228-31.

Stegman, Michael A. Housing Investment in the Inner City: The Dynamics of Decline. Cambridge, Mass.: MIT Press, 1972.

Sternlieb, George. The Myth and Potential Reality of Urban Home-
    steading. New Brunswick, N.J.: Rutgers University. Center for
    Urban Policy Research, 1974.

_____.Residential Abandonment: The Tenement Landlord Revisited.
    New Brunswick, N.J.: Rutgers University, Center for Urban
    Policy Research, 1973.

_____;Beaton, W. Patrick; Burchell, Robert W.; Hughes, James W.;
    James, Franklin J.; Listokin, David; and Windsor, Duane. Housing
    Development and Municipal Costs. New Brunswick, N.J.: Rutgers
    University, Center for Urban Policy Research, 1973.

_____;Burchell, Robert W.; Hughes, James W.; and James, Franklin J.
    "Housing Abandonment in the Urban Core." Journal of American
    Institute of Planners, September 1974, p. 321-32.

Stone, Lewis B. "An Urban Homestead Act." Current, March 1973,
    pp. 3-5.

"Urban Homesteading." Architectural Forum 139 (December 1973): 75.

"Urban Homesteading." Municipal Attorney 14, no. 10 (October 1973):
    196, 216.

"Urban Homesteading Pros, Cons Aired at Conference." Journal of
    Housing, May 1975, p. 228.

U.S. Department of Housing and Urban Development, ed. Abandoned
    Housing Research: A Compendium.Washington, D.C.: U.S. Gov-
    ernment Printing Office, 1973.

Wedemeyer, Dee. "Urban Homesteading." Nation's Cities, January
    1975, pp. 19-20.

Weicher, John C. "A Test of Jane Jacobs' Theory of Successful
    Neighborhoods." Journal of Regional Science 13, no. 1 (April
    1973): 29-40.

Welfeld, Irving H. America's Housing Problem. Washington, D.C.:
    American Enterprise Institute for Policy Research, 1973.

Westbrook, Crawford C. "Downtown Renovation Doesn't Mean
    Destroying Everything and Starting Over." The American City,
    December 1972, pp. 65-68.

Wolman, Harold. Politics of Federal Housing. New York: Dodd, Mead and Co., 1971.

The Woodlawn Organization. The Woodlawn's Model Cities Plan. Northbrook, Ill.: Whitehall Co., 1970.

Zimmer, Basil G. Rebuilding Cities: The Effects of Displacement and Relocation on Small Business. Chicago: Quadrangle Books, 1964.

Zimmerman, Joseph F. "Neighborhoods and Citizen Involvement." Public Administration Review 32 (May 1972): 201-09.

METHODOLOGY SOURCES

Bauer, Rainald K., and Frank Meissner. "Structures of Mail Questionnaires: Test of Alternatives." Public Opinion Quarterly 27, no. 2 (Summer 1963): 307-11.

Boek, Walter E., and James H. Lade. "A Test of the Usefulness of the Post-Card Technique in a Mail Questionnaire Study." Public Opinion Quarterly 27, no. 2 (Summer 1963): 303-06.

Gibson, Frank K., and Hawkins, Brett W. "Interviews versus Questionnaires." American Behavioral Scientist 12 (September-October 1968): NS9-16.

Gullahorn, Jeanne E., and Gullahorn, John T. "An Investigation of the Effects of Three Factors on Response to Mail Questionnaires." Public Opinion Quarterly 27, no. 2 (Summer 1963): 294-96.

Hatry, Harry P., and Winnie, Richard E. Measuring the Effectiveness of Local Government Services. Washington, D.C.: Urban Institute, 1972.

Hayes, Samuel P., Jr. Evaluating Development Projects. New York: Unesco, 1969.

Hubbard, Alfred W. "Phrasing Questions." Journal of Marketing 15, no. 1 (July 1950): 48-56.

McDonagh, Edward C., and Rosenblum, Leon. "A Comparison of Mailed Questionnaires and Subsequent Structured Interviews." Public Opinion Quarterly 29, no. 1 (Spring 1965): 131-36.

Mindlin, Albert. "The Use of Social Indicators in Municipal Government." In Social Indicators and Marketing, edited by Robert L. Clevett and Jerry C. Olson. Chicago: American Marketing Association, 1974.

Parten, Mildred. Surveys, Polls and Samples: Practical Procedures. New York: Harper and Bros., 1950.

Plog, Stanley C. "Explanations for a High Return Rate on a Mail Questionnaire." Public Opinion Quarterly 27, no. 2 (Summer 1963): 297-302.

Pomeroy, Mardell B. "The Reluctant Respondent." Public Opinion Quarterly 27, no. 2 (Summer 1963): 287-93.

Robins, Lee N. "The Reluctant Respondent." Public Opinion Quarterly 27, no. 2 (Summer 1963): 276-86.

Roeher, G. Allen. "Effective Techniques in Increasing Response to Mailed Questionnaires." Public Opinion Quarterly 27, no. 2 (Summer 1963): 299-302.

Ross, H. Lawrence. "The Inaccessible Respondent: A Note on Privacy in City and Country." Public Opinion Quarterly 27, no. 2 (Summer 1963): 267-75.

Rossi, Peter Henry. Evaluating Social Programs. New York: Seminar Press, 1972.

Vidich, Arthur J.; Joseph Bensman; and Maurice R. Stein. Reflections on Community Studies. New York: Harper and Row, 1964.

Weiss, Carol H., and Harry P. Hatry. An Introduction to Sample Surveys for Government Managers. Washington, D.C.: Weber Institute, 1971.

Wholey, Joseph S.; Scanlon, John W.; Duffy, Hugh G.: Fukumoto, James S.; and Vost, Leona M. Federal Evaluation Policy. Washington, D.C.: Urban Institute, 1973.

MAGAZINE AND NEWSPAPER ARTICLES

"Aid for Homeowner in Financial Need." Norfolk Journal and Guide, 31 May 1975.

Aldag, Karen. "Homesteaders, 1975: They Turn to Cities." New York
    Sunday Times - Union, 21 September 1975, p. F1.

Anderson, Jean. "You Can Buy a House for $1—Yes, $1!" Family
    Circle, April 1975, pp. 90-91, 128, 130.

Baynes, Susanne. "96 Good Reasons Why You Should Consider Moving
    Back into the City." St. Louisan, January 1974, pp. 15-16, 31.

Bronson, Gail. "The Old Homestead." Wall Street Journal, 21
    September 1973.

Crinklaw, Don. "What This City Needs Is Some Good $1 Houses."
    St. Louisan, January 1974, pp. 13-15.

Department of Urban Affairs, AFL-CIO. Housing Newsletter, 31
    October 1973, p. 2.

"Drive to Curb 'Redlining' in Run-down Neighborhoods." U.S. News
    and World Report, 9 June 1975, pp. 76-77.

"Editorial." Norfolk Ledger-Star, 20 September 1973.

"Editorial." Norfolk Virginian-Pilot, 22 September 1973, p. A 10.

"Editorial." Washington Post, 25 September 1973.

"Editorial." Washington Post, 10 July 1973.

Epstein, Aaron. "Homestead Plan Approved." Philadelphia Inquirer,
    20 July 1973.

Farrell, William E. "F.H.A. Mortgages Renounced as Path to
    Windfalls." New York Times, 15 July 1975.

_____."Redlining, Whether Cause of Effect, Is No Help." New York
    Times, 14 September 1975, p. E 2.

Fried, Joseph P. "Housing for Poor: Is it a Failure?" New York
    Times, 16 September 1973.

"Ghetto Homesteaders." Time, 13 August 1973, p. 6.

Halverson, Guy. "Free Homes in Inner City." Baltimore Sun,
    17 June 1973.

____."1,000 Inquiries for $1 Houses." Baltimore Sun, 14 October
     1973, p. F 1.

Holzhauer, Greg. "The Urban Homesteaders." The St. Louisan,
     May 1974, pp. 28-29.

"Homesteading in 1973—City Houses for $1." U.S. News and World
     Report, 5 November 1973, pp. 43-44.

"HUD's Hills Stresses Neighborhood Priorities." Washington Post,
     7 June 1975, p. E. 14.

"HUD Will Test Homesteading in 10 Urban Areas This Summer."
     New York Times, 31 May 1975, sec. 13, p. 5.

King, Wayne. "Homesteaders Combating Urban Blight." New York
     Times, 16 September 1973, p. A 1.

____."Urban Homesteading Faltering in Fight against Blight of
     Cities." New York Times, 30 May 1975, p. C 1.

Lippman, Thomas W. "The Urban Homestead—A New Kind of Fron-
     tier." Norfolk Virginian-Pilot, 17 February 1974.

Matthews, Linda. "HUD Benefits Untapped in Uninsured Areas."
     Washington Post, 26 July 1975, p. D 1.

Owen, Wilfred. "Planned Cities Make 'Downtown' Nice Place to
     Live." Norfolk Virginian-Pilot, 14 March 1974, p. D 15.

Ronis, Benjamin. "Abandoned Homes Given for Promise to Renovate."
     Washington Post, 22 September 1973, p. E 18.

Saar, Jon. "D.C. Frontiers, Inner-City Renewal Project, Will Open
     Soon." Washington Post, 13 August 1973, p. C. 1.

Spaulding, Theodore, Jr. Homestead Program Director. Personal
     Letter, 1 April 1975.

Tatro, Nick. "Urban Homesteaders Pay with Sweat. " Norfolk Ledger-
     Star, 14 March 1975.

Todd, Dean. "David Lodens Become First New Rockford Home-
    steaders." Rockford (Ill.) Register-Republic, 21 March 1975.

"Urban Homesteading—Saving Old Housing is the Name of the Claim."
    Savings and Loan News 95 (January 1974): 50-54.

"Using Homesteaders to Restore Cities." Business Week, 1 September
    1973, pp. 22-24.

Von Eckardt, Wolf. "Renewed, Vacant and Vandalized." Washington
    Post, 28 June 1975, p. C 2.

Wallace, C. David. "Restoration Emphasized by HUD in New Grants
    for Cities, Suburbs." Washington Post, 7 June 1975, p. E 1.

Waller, Linda. "People Are Making It Work." Norfolk, Virginian-
    Pilot, 26 January 1975, p. C 1.

Wilmann, John B. "An Approach to Low-Cost Housing." Washington
    Post, 27 October 1973, p. F 1.

ANNE CLARK is an urban sociologist. She has concentrated on the problems of the urban family and has done extensive community work with different family agencies and service organizations. She has a B.A. in sociology from the University of Texas. She has also studied at Stephens College and the University of Maryland. Sensing a need for urban programs to revitalize the cities, she pursued her master's degree in urban studies from Old Dominion University. She concentrated on urban problems and their sociological effects on urban dwellers. Urban disinvestment and rehabilitative housing programs became a major area of interest. There being no empirical studies on urban homesteading, this study was developed.

ZELMA RIVIN is chairman of the planning commission in Portsmouth, Virginia. She has been deeply involved in the problems of that urban core city for many years. She served on the school board for six years and for 25 years on various social, educational, and human-rights committees. She received her bachelor's degree from Northwestern University and has also studied at Ohio State University and the University of Virginia.

Concern for the future of urban America motivated her to enroll in the first class of urban studies at Old Dominion University. She was awarded a master's degree in urban studies in December 1975. Her studies in that program focused on housing problems, particularly in relation to urban disinvestment and to the political variables that affected them. Homesteading in Urban U.S.A. resulted from two years of research which she initiated when the first urban-homestead ordinance was passed.

Ms. Rivin and Ms. Clark have maintained active files on all homesteading programs since that time. Both Ms. Rivin and Ms. Clark submitted this study as a master's thesis in December 1975. Since that time, Ms. Rivin and Ms. Clark have written several articles. One, "Urban Homesteading Confronts Diverse Needs," was published in the July 1976 issue of National Civic Review. Another, "Administrative Models of Urban Homesteading," was published by Public Administration Review in early 1977.

At present Ms. Clark and Ms. Rivin are both instructors at Tidewater Community College.

HOUSING COSTS AND HOUSING NEEDS
edited by
Alexander Greendale
Stanley F. Knock, Jr.

HOUSING FINANCE AGENCIES: A Comparison between
States and HUD
Nathan S. Betnun

HOUSING MARKET PERFORMANCE IN THE UNITED
STATES
Charles J. Stokes
Ernest M. Fisher

HOUSING MARKETS AND CONGRESSIONAL GOALS
Ernest M. Fisher

HOUSING TURNOVER AND HOUSING POLICY: Case
Studies of Vacancy Chains in New York State
Gary Sands
Lewis L. Bower

NEIGHBORHOOD CHANGE: Lessons in the Dynamics
of Urban Decay
Charles L. Leven
James T. Little
Hugh O. Nourse
R. B. Read

THE POLITICS OF HOUSING IN OLDER URBAN AREAS
edited by
Robert E. Mendelson
Michael A. Quinn

PUBLIC HOUSING AND URBAN RENEWAL: An Analysis
of Federal-Local Relations
Richard D. Bingham